Richard Champion

Comparative Reflections on the Past and Present

Political, Commercial, and Civil State of Great Britain

Richard Champion

Comparative Reflections on the Past and Present
Political, Commercial, and Civil State of Great Britain

ISBN/EAN: 9783337134136

Printed in Europe, USA, Canada, Australia, Japan

Cover: Foto ©Suzi / pixelio.de

More available books at **www.hansebooks.com**

COMPARATIVE REFLECTIONS

ON THE PAST AND PRESENT

POLITICAL, COMMERCIAL, AND CIVIL STATE

OF

GREAT BRITAIN:

WITH SOME

THOUGHTS CONCERNING EMIGRATION.

BY RICHARD CHAMPION, Esq.
LATE DEPUTY PAYMASTER GENERAL OF HIS MAJE-
STY'S FORCES, AND AUTHOR OF CONSIDERATIONS
ON THE SITUATION OF GREAT BRITAIN WITH RE-
SPECT TO THE UNITED STATES OF AMERICA.

Scito mihi unquam fuisse tam infame, tam turpe, tam peræque omnibus generibus, ordinibus, ætatibus offensum, quam hunc statum qui nunc est. — Certe sumus periisse omnia: Quid enim ἀκκιζόμεθα tamdiu? Sed hæc scripsi properans, et mehercule timide.   CIC. ad ATT.

LONDON:
Printed for J. DEBRETT, in PICCADILLY.
M,DCC,LXXXVII.

CONTENTS.

LETTER I.

Page

CONTAINING the Author's motives for leaving England, and a general Introduction to thefe Reflections, - - - - - 3

II.

On the National Debt and Peace Eſtabliſhment, and on the State of the Government contraſted at different periods, - - - - - 19

III.

Upon the new Syſtem of Government introduced in the prefent Reign, - - - - - 37

IV.

On the ſtate and principles of the different Parties, the prevalence of the new Syſtem, and the difpoſition of the People to fubmit to it, 55

LETTER

LETTER V.

Upon the Coalition; the motives of the Whig leaders in forming it; and the event which followed, - - - - - - - - 69

VI.

Explanation of the apparent contradiction in the actions of the principal Whig leaders with respect to America, at two different periods of time, - - - - - - - - - - 89

VII.

The same subject continued, - - - - - 109

VIII.

On the necessity of vesting the Administration of Government in an able and vigorous Minister, - - - - - - - - - - 127

IX.

On the state of the Commerce of Great Britain before the War, - - - - - - - - 147

X.

On the state of the Commerce of Great Britain since the Peace, - - - - - - - - 165

LETTER XI.
                                        Page
Upon the former and present state of the manners of the People of Great Britain, - 189

XII.

The continuation of the same subject; chiefly upon the change which the East-India wealth produced in our manners, - - - 201

XIII.

The same subject continued; particularly with respect to the influence which the Newspapers have had in corrupting our manners, 215

XIV.

The subject concluded. The manners of Rome and London compared, and the danger shewn to which the latter is exposed, - 233

XV.

Upon Emigration, - - - - - - - - 251

XVI.

The subject of Emigration continued; particularly with respect to situation, - - - 269

XVII.

The same subject continued. The employments of Emigrants in America, - - - - 283

LETTER XVIII.

The same subject continued; upon those persons about the Court who will probably leave England, - - - - - - - - - - 301

XIX.

The same subject continued; upon the different ranks of people who will probably leave England, - - - - - - - - - - 319

XX.

The same subject continued. The situation of the first and present settlers of America contrasted; and the whole concluded, - 335

REFLECTIONS,

LETTER I.

CONTAINING

THE AUTHOR'S MOTIVES

FOR

LEAVING ENGLAND,

AND A

GENERAL INTRODUCTION

TO

THESE REFLECTIONS.

Fortuna sævo læta negotio, et
Ludum insolentem ludere pertinax,
Transmutat incertos honores
    Nunc mihi, nunc alii benigna.
Laudo manentem. Si celeras quatit
Pennas, resigno quæ dedit, et meo
Virtute me involvo, probamque
    Pauperiem sine dote quæro.
                        HOR.

REFLECTIONS, &c.

LETTER I.

TO ―――――

THE affairs of Great Britain, which have been for many years in a dangerous situation, are now advancing rapidly to a crisis. I do not remember any period in her history, since she has called herself a great nation, which has afforded so many solid grounds of apprehension for the event. As an individual, anxiously concerned for her welfare, I feel a most sensible regret, when I reflect how closely she has brought herself to the precipice of irrecoverable ruin,

ruin. Guiltless of her follies, having performed my duty to her as a subject, and finding my own particular situation so much involved in the late political events, as to render my private duties incompatible with a longer continuance under her government, I conceive myself fully justified in the resolution which I have now taken. These duties, urging me to a timely and provident care of a heavy charge which lies upon me, made me think it prudent to put in execution a plan which the infatuated system of government in my native country has long prepared me for, and which has, therefore, been the frequent subject of my serious thoughts.

It is a happiness, which is the envied lot of English Whigs, that there is a country, inhabited by Englishmen, once fellow subjects, and always dear to them, where the laws, the language, and the manners, will preserve constantly in her remembrance, the state of their native country in her best days. I am going to take refuge in in this country with a numerous family. I do it thus early, left the difficulties, already great in England, should increase to such a degree, as to make the removal of a family unpleasant and inconvenient.

I have been long desirous of paying a visit to America. During the year 1783, I had the fullest expectation of accomplishing my purpose, and of appearing there in a station which, affording me the powerful means of exerting very zealous endeavours for the restoration of the lost affections of that country, would have gratified my highest wishes. I perceived, with grateful feelings, the wishes of the citizens of the United States to cast the veil of oblivion over the violently impolitic and exasperating scenes which had passed, and to renew the friendly attachment of ancient times.

I therefore, at an early period after the peace, (immediately on the administration of the Duke of Portland being declared)

solicited

solicited the honourable station of Consul to the United States. I had, by an assiduous attention to the affairs of America for above twenty years, obtained a very considerable knowledge of the resources of that country. Conceiving, therefore, my abilities not to be ill adapted to this station, I had the confidence to believe that I should not in any shape have discredited the appointment.

I considered myself, in another view, not to be an improper (I might, perhaps, have proved an useful) person in such an employment. My conduct during every stage of the late unhappy disputes had been decided and consistent. I always acted with the strictest regard to the true interests of both nations, in supporting, by all possible means within my powers and abilities, those measures which tended either to preserve the affairs of America upon its ancient system, to prevent the late unnatural war, to impede its monstrous and destructive growth, or to promote

mote the return of peace. I had reason, therefore, to expect the most friendly reception.

When a negociation for a treaty of commerce (if it merit the name, since it miscarried so early as to leave almost a doubt of its conception) was first mentioned, and I had been made acquainted with the intention of Administration to appoint me Consul to the United States, the Minister did me the honour to put some papers relative to the American trade into my hands, with a desire to have my sentiments upon them. I collected my own papers on that subject, which I arranged during the summer of 1783, and drew up considerations on the commercial connections of the two countries, with a view of throwing every possible light upon the subject, for the information of Government. These I presented to the Minister. But as the Administration was soon after changed, I thought it proper, expecting that it would shortly become the object of parliamentary deliberation, to offer them to the public. I have since added a proposed act of parliament, which, I am justified in saying, from the opinion of men of the first abilities, knowledge, and integrity, is adapted to the true interests of both countries, and to which no reasonable objections can be made.

I have met with the fate of many others who have trodden the same path. The consciousness of having done my duty has been the only reward of my labours. It has not, however, been the only return; for I have had the end of these very labours, founded upon principles in which the prosperity of Great Britain was most essentially concerned, either grossly misunderstood, or grossly perverted. They have been mentioned by men, now in high stations, as the objections (it was civilly added, the only ones that could be made) to my filling the appointment which had been designed for me. I do not know whether the censures which have been thrown

thrown upon me, for the sentiments contained in that work, merit my attention, or render the few observations which I shall make upon them at all necessary: but I can confidently say, trusting to the rectitude of my intentions, and to innocency of design, either to do injury myself, or to be the cause of it to any person whatever, that I hear these censures unmoved.

By some I have been called an American agent. By one writer I am stiled, " the Apologist of Congress." If being an advocate for the rights of mankind—an advocate for peace—an advocate for the return of those good offices which formerly distinguished Great Britain and her Colonies — an advocate for the re-establishment of those measures which had raised the glory of England to an height unknown since that of the Romans was extinguished, is being a professed apologist for Congress, I acknowledge that I am one, and I glory in the title. If it be a crime

crime to have lamented over the measures which marked out for destruction those beautiful and rising colonies, which the fostering hand of Britain had raised for her grandeur and happiness, I am a criminal indeed. I would be an apologist if I could; but it should be for those measures which disgrace the annals of my native country; and which (perhaps this may be deemed a crime) I wish to see buried for ever in a cordial reconciliation.

Is it possible for any one, who, with the manly Gown, received those strong impressions of glory, which the victories of Englishmen fixed upon his youthful mind, and which have since been defaced in the dust—is it possible, I say, for such a person to part from England without the deepest regret?—The peace of 1763 had left her in possession of a name which was a passport through the globe. The peace of 1783 has left that name sunk, debased, and treated with contempt by every petty nation in Europe. Must I not,

not, therefore, leave my country with the moſt bitter reflections, who have been the melancholy ſpectator of this gloomy reverſe of fortune?

It was a mortification to me to be obliged to leave England before the winter. I was deprived by it of the ſatisfaction of taking leave of many valuable friends, whom the receſs of Parliament had diſperſed in their ſeveral counties. But ſuch was the diſguſting and ungentleman-like behaviour of my ſucceſſor in office, (a ſtrong proof from the obliging, though fruitleſs, interpoſition of his principal, of the wretched ſyſtem of controlling every man of rank in Adminiſtration) that I could not ſtay till the ſpring without very conſiderable trouble and expence. I was obliged, therefore, to deny myſelf this gratification.

The laſt ſight of the Britiſh ſhore ſunk deep into my heart, and left an impreſſion

sion which will not easily be erased. The evening we parted from it was serene, and the sun dipped his beams to the westward in a calm and unruffled ocean. The Lizard Point was in view.

Nos manet oceanus circumvagus.

For earth—surrounding sea our flight awaits.
Francis's Horace.

Peace and tranquillity sat upon the bosom of the vast Atlantic, and pointed out the way we were to go; whilst the gathering distant clouds, which hung over the land, seemed to tell us, that it was time to leave infatuated Britain. I tremble for you and for the excellent friends whom I have left behind me; and from whom, had I been a single individual, I could not without difficulty have torne myself: and I offer my most fervent prayers to that Almighty Being who holds the scale of empires, that your woes may be light; and that when our country comes in the approaching

ing crisis to be weighed in the balance, she may be so thoroughly purged from her dross, as to appear again with brighter lustre.

I owe to you, and to my friends, the opinions which I have formed upon the present situation of affairs in England, and upon which my conduct in leaving it was founded. I mean to offer to your consideration the present state of its government, of its trade, and of its manners; and, drawing a comparison between their present and former state, I shall endeavour to prove to you — that the government of Great Britain is deranged in such a manner, as to afford, in its present condition, little or no hope of remedy — that our commerce, which, like a candle going out, has just emitted a strong and fervid light, is groaning under such foreign and domestic burdens, as must inevitably reduce it to a very low state — and that the present stile of living in England is attended with

with such an enormous expence, without an adequate means of support, as to make the first national calamity a sure and certain sign of a great and general destruction of property amongst all ranks and distinctions of men.

From these considerations I shall shew the probability of a great emigration of its people, whom necessity will drive from home; and I shall then draw such useful inferences, as will, by a timely exertion of their present abilities, preserve them against the worst consequences of the storm.

I shall confine myself as closely as I can to plain matters of fact; forming such conclusions only as those facts will justify to the most common understanding. In this spirit, therefore, of plainness and simplicity, the most consistent with the manners of a republic, of which I hope soon to become a citizen; and taking my leave of all other titles and distinctions than

than those which arise from the honourable functions of magistracy, I content myself with offering you my most fervent wishes for your health and happiness, and bidding you heartily farewel.

From on board the Britannia, at sea,
   Oct. 20, 1784.

LETTER

LETTER II.

ON THE
NATIONAL DEBT AND PEACE ESTABLISHMENT,
AND ON THE
STATE OF THE GOVERNMENT
CONTRASTED AT DIFFERENT PERIODS.

But the establishment of public funds, on the credit of taxes, hath been productive of more and greater mischiefs than the taxes themselves; not only by increasing the means of corruption, and the power of the Crown, but by the effect it has had on the spirit of the nation, on our manners, and our morals. It is impossible to look back without grief, on the necessary and unavoidable consequence of this establishment; or without indignation on that mystery of iniquity *, to which this establishment gave occasion, which has been raised upon it, and carried on for almost half a century by means of it. It is impossible to look forward without horror on the consequences that may still follow.

Bolingbroke upon Parties.

---

* Stockjobbing.

LETTER II.

TO ―――――

I SHALL resume the subject of my last letter. The situation in which Great Britain was left at the peace of 1783, required the ablest and most settled administration that the country could produce. Such an administration was essentially necessary to her, in the condition to which she had been reduced by the late unfortunate war; one of the wretched consequences of the weak and disjointed system upon which she has been governed (a short period excepted) during the present reign.

But instead of a regular and settled government, administration has succeeded administration, like puppets at a show. About twenty months have passed since the

the peace. Within this short period there have been no less than three administrations, each acting upon principles diametrically opposite to the other. Frequent changes in government will materially injure even a flourishing country. To a nation, therefore, exhausted by a long and unsuccessful war, they must be productive of the most fatal consequences.

The plainest method of demonstrating this wretched state of the country, is, by the application of facts. For that purpose I shall begin with the year 1754, a period within the remembrance of the greater part of us, and continuing it to the present time, I shall form such occasional comparisons as are adapted to the subject.

The interest upon the national debt, and the expence of the peace establishment; the revenues of the customs and excise, and of the taxes, which were first, and have since been, imposed, to defray the charge of government, at different periods, will

will more diftinctly fhew the fituation of the country.

They were as follow:

	Debt. £.	Intereft. £.	The whole peace eftablifhment. £.	Increafe. £.
1754	75,000,000	2,650,000	6,500,000	
1774	136,000,000	4,200,000	10,000,000	3,500,000
1784	250,000,000	9,500,000	15,000,000	8,500,000

The increafe of the national debt, and of the additional burdens neceffary to difcharge the intereft, have produced the natural confequence — a decay of our credit, and a decreafe in value of our property. The price of the funds have funk, from about one hundred and five to lefs than fifty-five, during the period of which we are treating. They do not at prefent greatly exceed one half of their value in the year 1754. The careful father, who had laid out in the funds ten thoufand pounds, as a future provifion for his family, now feels a fenfible difappointment at the decreafe of their portion to the poor pittance of five thousand five hundred pounds. The income which it produced, of two hundred and eighty pounds per annum, then afforded him the comforts of life. At this time, when all our expences are extravagantly enhanced, they barely supply the necessaries. But his grievances are not confined to reduction of capital, and increase of expence; he is farther compelled to endure the additional national burden of upwards of nine millions per annum, accumulated taxes.

In giving this account of the exhausted and dangerous state of the kingdom, I am aware of one, though an ill-timed, objection, that may be urged against me. I may be told, that the same desponding language has been used in all periods in our history; and that there has seldom been a year in which volumes have not been written to prove, that our commerce was in a state of decay, and that our ruin stared us in the face: but the times in which we live are attended with very aggravated

gravated circumstances. We have sunk from an immense power and greatness. Our pangs are the pangs of a giant, torn to pieces by the violence of a fever raging in his veins. In the dreadful paroxisms of the disease, his whole frame is convulsed.

Though we have for many years outlived these predictions, yet our present situation proves, that they were formed upon very solid grounds. The fears of those who have written upon the subject, appear to have arisen from the state of the national debt. They saw the foundation laid for a building, which, though at first designed to be merely temporary, soon swelled to a great size, and is since become an immense structure. In a short time after its establishment, the national debt increased with a rapidity that left very little hope of seeing it paid off. An annual grant of taxes was made to the Crown, to defray the interest. This soon became perpetual. The view, therefore, of those who

who were thus apprehensive for posterity, was far from being imperfect. They felt the force of the school boy's reasoning, when he could not be prevailed upon to say A. The repetition of A produced the repetition of B, and we have at length been forced through the whole alphabet.

When the national debt became a permanent fund, and permanent taxes were laid to pay the interest, a speculation was made how much debt the public could bear without injury. One of our ministers conceived, from the then difficulty of finding resources, that the national debt could never exceed one hundred millions without a manifest injury to the public. He judged, probably, from the value of money. When the nation owed seventy-five millions, the funds bore a premium of five per cent.

In proportion as the debt increased, the premium decreased. This proves that one hundred millions of debt, at three per cent.

cent. per annum interest, which is the standard of our funds, would have made their value nearly the par of one hundred pounds. The national debt cannot, therefore, by a parity of reasoning, be extended beyond this limit, and the national prosperity at the same time maintained. Unless some acquisitions, either in commerce or dominion, compensated for a temporary increase, by putting us in a condition to discharge the surplus in time of peace.

Had the Government under the present reign been placed in able hands, the valuable acquisitions which were made in the war of 1756 would have effected this purpose. When the whole expences of that war were wound up, and the funds had recovered their peaceful tone, the three per cents., which is a low interest, and has been always considered as a profitable standard, settled at about ten per cent. under the par of one hundred. The advantages which these acquisitions produced,

duced, afford us sufficient grounds to suppose that had they been properly improved, the surplus debt might have been discharged, and the price of the funds increased to their standard value.

Their effects were very conspicuous in the general improvements of the kingdom, in its fertilised lands, in a great and extended commerce, and in a display of riches and magnificence in all orders of the State. What has been said upon this subject certainly proves, that had the surplus debt been paid off, the nation could have borne one hundred millions of debt, invested in permanent funds, without decreasing the value of money; and that every addition made to it is a loss, which falls upon the various branches of our property.

The effects of this national prosperity are still visible; and, although the sources from whence they sprung are nearly exhausted, the luxurious and expensive manner

ner of living which it produced, still remains. Sober men will reflect upon the means by which these expences are to be defrayed. They will consider the magnificence of our appearance, and the costliness of our tables, as mere stumbling blocks, which deceive our eyes, and corrupt our manners. They will naturally draw a comparison between the times when these riches were collected, and the present age, in which they are daily diminishing and melting away, and in which there is no other accumulation than that of expence.

In this examination they will find, that these riches were the production of a flourishing commerce, increased by a train of victories and conquests. They repaid in value the expence of the war, by the centering of almost the whole of the French trade in our ports — by the total destruction of the little that was left to France — by the annihilation of the naval power of the House of Bourbon — and by the possession

session of nearly their whole colonial empire, and a valuable part of that of Spain.

These great and glorious acquisitions, a great part of which was, and a much greater part of which might have been, retained at the peace of 1763, were purchased at the price of sixty-five millions of national debt; increasing the whole debt to about one hundred and forty millions, and making an excess of forty millions above the one hundred millions of debt, which the nation appeared to be capable of bearing without injury. This excess of forty millions of debt might, under an able administration of the great empire in our possession, have been in the course of a few years discharged.

Such is the examination of the times in which those riches which still remain among us were accumulated. We shall now enter into the consideration of those in which we live: but, how melancholy is the contrast!

We

We are now, as we were in the year 1763, at peace. Our Government is feeble and deraged. Our national debt, when the expences of the war are wound up, will be nearly doubled. The fruits of the glorious war of 1756 are almost wholly lost. Our ancient, powerful, and wonderfully-increasing colonies, forming an immense empire, are torn from us; and our remaining colonial possessions either in gradual decay, or in great and imminent danger. Our sister kingdom in a state of miserable confusion; whilst the mother country is bending under the pressure of more than fifteen millions, annually imposed upon her, to discharge the interest of her national debt, and to support her peace establishment.

If we inquire into the revenue from whence these fifteen millions ought to be drawn, we shall find it in the most precarious situation. This arises from the continual inroads made upon the customs and excise by the smuggler; from the decay of trade, occasioning many unproductive taxes; and from other contingent circumstances; consequences which usually happen to a nation in a declining condition.

It is the opinion of those most conversant in the revenue, that more than twelve millions cannot possibly be raised toward its discharge. The distress of an individual, and the distresses of the public, are equally destructive to them. They never borrow but with disadvantage; and never pay but with accumulated interest. Whatever deficiencies there are in the ways and means provided by Parliament, they must be borrowed, and fresh taxes must be raised to defray the interest: at least, the forms must be passed through; though it is scarcely possible to conceive, that the people can bear an addition to their present impositions.

It is much more probable, that they will be incapable of paying even those which are already exacted from them.
Govern-

Government muſt take great care that they do not, by weight of taxes, deſtroy the means from whence theſe taxes are to ariſe. If you want your horſes to be in good condition, and to labour hard, you muſt take care to feed them well. Should you deprive them of their oats, they will not be capable of doing much work.

The diſplay of our riches will ſerve with many for argument. Though it may be plauſible, it is very futile. The appearances of grandeur remain long after the reſources are gone, and the power which protects them is loſt. But there is one circumſtance which makes me very much doubt the exiſtence of ſo much real wealth, eſpecially in ſilver plate, as there was ſome years ago: this is the decreaſe of ſilver veſſels in families, and the very great increaſe of ſilver plated ones; the whole of which is an entire loſs to the ſtate. This branch of trade certainly requires conſideration.

But

But, suppofing that our empire was as extenfive, our commerce as flourifhing, and our revenues as fecure, as they were at the peace of 1763, ftill the charge of fifteen millions per annum would be found to be a very fevere burden; and if thus fevere in the heighth of profperity, how much more difficult muft it be for the nation to bear, in its prefent diftreffed condition?

I have given the ftate of the national debt, the annual revenue and taxes which are to be raifed for the payment of the intereft, and for the peace eftablifhment of the kingdom. I have not been able to infert the exact fractional fums, as I have not materials to recur to; I have, therefore, placed them in round numbers: but I venture confidently to affert, that thefe numbers are fo very near the precife fums, as to fatisfy every reafonable perfon. I have alfo formed a fhort comparative view of the former and prefent ftate of the nation, and the probability, not only of the people's incapacity to bear any frefh impofitions, positions, but even of the decrease of the present scanty revenue.

I shall in my next letter take a short view of the system of government which has prevailed under the present reign. — Farewel.

From on board the Britannia, at sea,
October 21, 1784.

LETTER III.

UPON THE
NEW SYSTEM OF GOVERNMENT
INTRODUCED IN THE
PRESENT REIGN.

Fert animus causas, tantarum expromere rerum,
Immensumque aperitur, opus quid in arma furentem
Impulerit populum, quid pacem excusserit orbi.

LUCAN.

THE practical system of government which has prevailed under the present reign, was originally arranged in the family of the late Princess Dowager of Wales, and carried into execution by the Earl of Bute on the King's accession to the throne. It has generated all the effects which the framers proposed to themselves; for it has shaken the confidence of family connections, weakened the habits of respect for Administration, totally destroyed the stability of Government, and finally been productive of all the calamities which have befallen the nation. The Administration has been bandied about in such a manner, that Government has neither grace nor vigour left in it: like a woman,

woman, whose beauty might have animated desire and commanded respect, when united with virtue, she begets loathing and excites contempt when deformed by prostitution.

We meet with many instances, even in those times when the Administration was stable and permanent, of ministers of a weak capacity for government. Such men were usually directed by some favourite, who exercised the power of his master, and generally with greater ability. The weakness of the minister might, perhaps, sometimes excite a smile within the circle of the Court. Still, as he possessed the actual power, he possessed the influence of his place, and had all the credit with the public, and preserved the respect due to his rank. But the smallest trace cannot be found of a minister who had the meanness to submit to be governed by some secretary, expressly placed about his person as a spy upon his actions, in order to retain his obedience to a cabal in the closet,

closet, who are the *efficient*, though they have neither rank nor consequence to form even the ostensible, Administration.

In the first instance, should a minister be directed by his favourite, it is yet a favourite of his own creation, and does not derogate from his general consequence in the eyes of the public. He can resume the power which he delegates whenever he thinks proper; but, in the latter case, the ostensible minister is a mere tool, a stage puppet, acting at the discretion of another, without will or opinion of his own. Since the introduction of the new system, we have seen this management of ministers practised in almost every department of Government. Every great officer of state has a secratary, or deputy, imposed upon him. A Lord Lieutenant of Ireland is under the same tutelage. The place of first minister has yet stronger guards.

The ostensible ministers are, in general, confined to the care of the several departments,

ments, and are made responsible alone for them. The cabal too prevalently keeps, for the important purposes of Government, some secretary about the person of the First Lord of the Treasury to receive their orders: and, on the like occasions, some invisible, though powerful, agent to manifest their pleasure. The ostensible ministers are not only directed to obey their commands, when signified in this manner, but have frequently suffered the disgrace of having measures imposed upon them in the House of Commons, without any previous communication with them.

The characteristic of almost every Administration under this reign has been an heterogeneous mixture of debility and insolence, tyranny and corruption. Lord Rockingham and the Duke of Portland, who governed during the very short periods of their administration, upon the old system, are the only exceptions. And, in general, the councils more immediately attendant upon the Crown, have been actuated

actuated by these principles, in opposition to the system of Administration carried on under the reigns of the two first princes of the Brunswick family. These two systems have been called by a variety of names. By some they have been thus distinguished: the one by that of a prerogative, the other by that of an aristocratical government. I will endeavour to explain the principles of each.

The system which prevailed under the two first reigns of this family was the same that has been since distinguished by the name of an aristocratical government. The Administration was selected from the principal Whig families, who all concurred in the support of the person placed at the head of the Treasury, to whom they were generally united by long habits of attachment. All the other officers were made properly subordinate to, and dependent upon, his department. They yielded to him the rank of first minister, and shewed an example to their fellow subjects

subjects in the deference and respect which they paid to him.

Under this system, that excellent maxim in the Constitution, " the King can do no " wrong," was holden sacred. This doctrine, essentially necessary to a Whig government, which considers the King as not performing any act in his own person, makes all his ministers responsible for every measure which they execute in his name. Were it, therefore, possible that the King should require the execution of any measure inconsistent with the public welfare, it is the minister who executes, and not the King who directs, that is responsible. Every minister is thus responsible in his department; but as the first minister has the management of the supplies of money granted by the House of Commons, more particularly entrusted to his care, and as he is by common consent the chief administrator, he is considered particularly responsible for all the measures of government.

This

This system was maintained by a combination of the whole of the landed property, and all the great family interests of the Whigs, as well as by the principal monied men. Extensive connections amongst the people produced an active and vigorous support of the measures of government: and, being possessed of power, all those who were swayed by interest, which has considerable weight amongst a commercial people, were attached to Administration. As the minister grounded his strength upon a majority in the House of Commons, his friends were solicitous that this influence should pervade all parts of the kingdom, particularly those places which returned members to Parliament.

Whilst the minister remained in possession of this strength in Parliament, it was not in the power of the Crown, without the utmost difficulty, to displace him. The loss of this majority was owing to the increase of the opposition to him in the House of Commons; either from his own

ill

ill conduct, or from some unpopular measure, with the weight of which his opponents overpowered him.

A strong opposition in Parliament was then considered as an accessary help to the Constitution; a necessary control over the measures of the minister. The Opposition was, therefore, no sooner become the majority of the House of Commons, than the minister was supposed incapable, from guilt or inability, and his resignation followed in course. The withstanding the power of the House of Commons was a phenomenon reserved for more unhappy times.

During the period of which we have been speaking there were no ministers of very striking abilities; and there were some, who, in their capacity for government, were remarkably deficient; yet, from the long and steady habits which are essential to a good government, the country had a continual increase of wealth
and

and vigour till it attained to the firſt rank of power and influence in Europe. Theſe habits of a ſettled government are not eaſily deſtroyed. The Whigs, having been in poſſeſſion of the adminiſtration for near fifty years, were ſo much maſters of the elections, that, notwithſtanding almoſt all the Parliaments of this reign have acted in obedience to the new ſyſtem, they have conſiſted more of apoſtate Whigs than of real Tories.

This was the ſyſtem of government carried on under the reigns of the Kings George the Firſt and George the Second. It muſt be goading to royalty to be thus continually fettered: but it muſt at the ſame time be confeſſed by even its moſt ſtrenuous ſupporters, that there never was a period of our hiſtory, taking it in a general view from the acceſſion of the Brunſwick kings, of greater national proſperity.

To deftroy this fyftem of government has been too uniformly and too eagerly attempted. The prefent King mounted the throne with many qualities, which engaged the affections of his fubjects. He was young, born amongft them, of a grave and fedate turn, and wholly free from the diffipated manners of the young men of this age. He married, grew fond of a domeftic life; his chief pleafures appearing to be centered in his family. Such virtues of the man, joined to the virtues of the king, muft always prove highly eftimable. The firft qualities, however, will conftantly endear a monarch to his people. His favourites did not neglect this difpofition.

The Court breathed nothing but complaints againft the ariftocratical thraldom in which both King and people were faid to be confined. They cried out loudly upon the neceffity of a prince of fuch hopes, being actually vefted with the administration

ministration of his own affairs. He would then, they said, be able to distinguish men of virtue and talents, and to open the door to those qualities which an unjust combination of a few families of great parliamentary interest had shut up for the use alone of themselves and their dependents.

By fomenting the prejudices and provoking the passions of those men who composed the administration of George the Second, at the time of his death; by intrigues in families; by liberal promises of rewards, adapted to the several desires of those upon whom they thus practised, the Court, at length, established the truth of the maxim, " to divide is to command." They received all those who came over to them with open arms. By the accomplishment of this principle, they established the new system of government. The former steady and permanent system was thus gradually put an end to. The regularity of manners, which had distinguished

guished the period of the two preceding reigns, insensibly followed.

The effect of this conduct soon appeared in the House of Commons. The sacred bonds of friendship and relative connections were broken down. Desertion from party became frequent. And such were the suspicions which prevailed, in consequence, amongst the remaining members in opposition, that, before the great event of the American war took place, the immediate friends of Lord Rockingham alone remained. When they were collected together, they amounted to seventy or eighty members: but their hopes were so slender from that Parliament in which the Boston Port bill, the prelude to the war, passed, that they seldom appeared together. Upon that important question, the opposition to it consisted only of the friends of that nobleman, who were men of business, and generally attended the House. Colonel Barré, Mr. Dunning, and the friends of Lord L. either absented themselves

themselves or voted for the bill. The whole number against it, as far as I can now recollect, was thirty-four.

The secret junto were now masters of both ministers and opposition. They had constantly a strong body of members in the House, composed of those who had places in the household, the secretaries or deputies of men in office, or of such others who were their immediate dependents. These were called King's friends. This body was under some known leader of the junto, who made use of frequent opportunities to shew the House the absolute dependence which the ostensible ministers had upon them.

Constantly using the precaution of selecting for the members of Administration such men as had few connections, the junto retained within themselves the entire direction of the affairs of Government. They will always find ministers to execute their measures of sufficient rank to give some grace to Administration, though not of connections sufficient to render their power dangerous.

In the midst of caresses, the Court did not neglect its security. No sooner was a proselyte made, than he was required to make his recantation public by some striking action; perhaps some parliamentary motion in direct opposition to his former principles. Two purposes were answered by this conduct. It secured the proselyte, at least as far as such a man could be secured, by the entire loss of reputation. And it not only destroyed the confidence which the people had placed in public characters, but greatly weakened the opinion which they held of the sanctity of family connections. The principles of men in general were then known by these connections. Where, at present, can we find a standard by which any judgement may be formed, except amongst the family of *Cavendish?*

People in a monarchy are naturally envious of thofe perfons who are invefted with public employments: but this paffion is not without a mixture of fear and refpect. The poffibility of their wanting the affiftance of men in power produces the former paffion. The poffeffion of the place procures refpect to it, as their envy is attended with a ftrong defire to enjoy it themfelves. The Court have been long endeavouring to ftrengthen this difpofition by inculcating the doctrine, that a candidate for places and power has intereft alone in view; and that patriotifm exifts only in the imagination. They have fupported thefe doctrines by fuch ftriking examples in men of the firft rank, that it would have been a miracle had not the opinion prevailed.

I have not only wearied myfelf by the unpleafant picture which I have drawn, but I fhall too much tranfgrefs the bounds of a letter by a longer continuance of the subject:

subject: I shall, therefore, defer it for the present. Farewel.

From on board the Britannia, at sea,
Oct. 23, 1784.

LETTER

LETTER IV.

ON THE STATE AND PRINCIPLES OF THE DIFFERENT PARTIES, THE PREVALENCE OF THE NEW SYSTEM, AND THE DISPOSITION OF THE PEOPLE TO SUBMIT TO IT.

A free people may be sometimes betrayed; but no people will betray themselves, and sacrifice their liberty, unless they fall into a state of universal corruption; and when they are fallen into such a state, they will be sure to lose what they deserve no longer to enjoy.

Bolingbroke upon Parties.

LETTER IV.

TO ——————

FROM the annals of history too well may we become convinced that it is a harsh and ungrateful language in the ears of kings, educated in the lap of power, and accustomed to be approached with deference and adulation, to recommend a system of government which derogates from their authority; more especially, when this system constitutes a House of Commons, the representatives of the people, to be the primary object, to whom his ministers must in all cases defer, and from whom alone they can derive the necessary support to the administration of his government. Princes would grow naturally jealous of a popular assembly, were it proved to have prescribed bounds which their succeffor could not venture to pass. They find, under this system, the royal power to be a mighty name in apparent possession of high prerogative, but which is rendered useless by the impossibility of procuring a servant hardy enough to execute his orders.

But are we not to suppose that this has been the condition of the prerogative since the Revolution, and particularly during the reigns of the first Brunswick kings, in whose hands every part of the royal prerogative, that formerly excited apprehension, was suffered by their ministers quietly to rest? Must we not consider such a conduct as tending equally to advance the happiness and improvement of the country? And would not attempts to bring them generally into practice, or, to carry the supposition farther, a violent exertion of a principal branch of the prerogative, prove the melancholy reverse?

The

The Whig party has been the moſt ſtrenuous ſupporters of the old ſyſtem. They have alſo been equally ſtrenuous ſupporters of the preſent family upon the throne. The pretenſions of the exiled prince of the Stuart race, to whom the Tories were zealouſly attached, made it a point of neceſſity for the two firſt kings of this family to put the adminiſtration of government into the hands of the Whigs. The non-exerciſe of many parts of the prerogative, which had been aſſerted with a jealous right by the Stuart kings, ſometimes proved the ſtrength of their feelings; but having no means of redreſs, they had no remedy but ſubmiſſion, the hardeſt taſk that a prince can feel. They, however, had the ſatisfaction of beholding this trial of their feelings more than repaired by the increaſing proſperity of their people.

The Tories, on the contrary, being ſtrongly attached to kingly prerogative, have always acted upon oppoſite principles. They conſidered the conduct of the

Whig

Whig ministers, in restraining the exercise of any branch of the prerogative, as an insult offered to the regal dignity. They were apprehensive that from the non-usage of any particular part, the legality of exercising it might, in the course of time, be called in question; and feared that a claim, founded upon prescriptive right, would be in future opposed to every attempt of the Crown to revive it: thus rendering it a service of great danger to the minister who should be sufficiently hardy to make the attempt.

These objections of the Tories do not appear to have been made without some grounds; for when Lord L. revived the doctrine of the lawfulness of the King's negative in Parliament, the right was immediately questioned: yet who, in his senses, can suppose that this was, probably, designed to be the prologue to a play, then in rehearsal? Who can presume even slightly to infer that the first scene has been performed? Or that the remaining

remaining part may follow at a future season?

Little, indeed, would the Tories of the present day have to fear, were it possible that a British throne could become besieged by any secret junto inclined to prompt a king to exertions for the resumption of the ancient prerogative of the Tudor and Stuart race.

Have we no reason to fear that the people of England experience a considerable decrease of that plain sense and blunt honesty by which they were formerly distinguished? The change of living within these last twenty years has produced an entire change of manners. Their natural jealousy, susceptible of the smallest national affront, has totally forsaken them. The ill success which attended the violent measures of Government in the late war, and to which the whole body of the Tories, and a great number of infatuated Whigs, granted their support, has had very

very melancholy effects upon their difpofition. They have fallen into habits of the moſt unbecoming meanneſs. There is hardly a man to be found who is not, by inclination or neceffity, a dependent on Government, or who has not a hope to procure for himſelf, or his couſin's couſin to the tenth generation, a place or a contract. Dependence naturally produces fervility of mind, and deadens a people to every fenfe of proper feeling.

A prince may be himſelf deceived by a popular deluſion, raiſed by artful and deſigning men, for their own purpoſes. He may be led into evils which may prove, in the event, of a magnitude beyond the power of redreſs. His own intention may be merely to refume thoſe prerogative rights which, according to the doctrines of his Tory ſubjects, he conceives to be the legal rights of the Crown. But could any prince, except our own, when he proceeds, and finds the people diſpoſed to ſubmiſſion, take upon him to anſwer for himſelf, that

that he shall be able to resist the temptation of assuming an absolute dominion over subjects who thus court his power?

Happy, happy Great Britain! where it is not possible to find even the slightest reason for supposing that a similar Revolution might be effected, in the present temper of the people, though not perhaps with the same ease, as that of Sweden, yet without any material resistance. Injustice alone could dare to propagate an idea that the Swedish Revolution was highly extolled at Court; or that it was not unusual to hear men of consideration say, "A mild "despotic government is much preferable "to the turbulence of party: our pro- "perty will be more secure."

Could (but the idea is absurd) such a disposition of the people take place, it must prove of little consequence to inquire of what party they were composed. Their general corruption would lead them equally to join in the same servile act of submission.

submission. Who can become so infatuated as to believe that the far greater part of the English are Tories, strongly attached to arbitrary power? If, by the word republicanism, we mean a regard for the public safety, an attachment to the common weal, to the *res publica*, such as it may, and even should exist under a monarchy, I wish, for the honour of the nation, (and upon this ground only do I form the wish) that there were more republicans in England. It would then contain a still-more virtuous people.

Some, inclined to these sentiments, are amongst the supporters of a parliamentary reform. I do honour to their hearts; for I believe their intentions to be upright and sincere. But I cannot do honour, in this instance, to their understandings, nor to any men who have the weakness to suppose that, in the present age, they would, in general, find electors of purity and integrity. Were the greater part of the nation

tion Tories, whose opinions approach very near to arbitrary government, and were the greater part also of the Whigs to apostatize from their principles, I must confess that, in such a case, far, very far indeed from probable, the future consequences would dreadfully alarm the well-wishers of their country.

And yet I do not recollect a more striking appearance of a change of disposition in the people than in the suspension of the Habeas-Corpus Act during the American war. Whilst every person conceived himself to be in danger, a general apprehension prevailed: but when an amendment was moved to the bill, extending the suspension only to those who had been out of the kingdom, this general apprehension subsided; and the man who found himself to be in no danger from it, turned a deaf ear to the difficulties in which his neighbours might be involved.

The

The then Administration, indeed, came readily into the amendment: and yet who shall say that it exactly coincided with the maxims of any system, framed to indulge subjects in all manner of licentiousness? Yet such is personal liberty when abused; for, by these means, their morals would be the sooner corrupted; consequently rendered subservient to the purposes of any future government, not losing sight of the grand and baneful objects with which the exceptionable reigns of former times have generally commenced — the diminution of the liberty of the subject, and the increase of the power and influence of the Crown.

Men of arbitrary principles are very severe in their dispositions: and such would introduce a new system with violence and malignity; yet they would find the English to be a people who may be led, but cannot easily be driven. A junto must meet with such difficulties in their vehement progress, that they would think it
most

most prudent to change their mode of attack, and to proceed by sap rather than by storm. They would attempt to debauch their manners. Yet why these odious suppositions? Surely we have never seen the success attending their levelling all distinction of character amongst men; nor that, as one part of their new doctrine was to annihilate private character, they inculcated the principle, that public virtue might exist independently of private. Could such absurdities become greedily swallowed by the people? By such means, indeed, might the manners of the people become loosened, and, by degrees, totally changed.

In my next I shall make some reflections, in continuation of this subject, upon those Whigs who have deserted their principles: till then I bid you farewel.

From on board the Britannia, at sea,
    Oct. 25, 1784

LETTER V.

UPON THE
COALITION,
THE
MOTIVES OF THE WHIG LEADERS
IN FORMING IT,
AND THE
EVENT WHICH FOLLOWED.

Quid verius quam in judicium venire, que ob re judicandam pecuniam acceperit? Censuit hoc Cato. — Quid impudenter publicanis renuntiantibus? Fuit tamen retinendi ordinis causa, facienda jactura.

Cic. ad Att.

THE general conduct of the two parties in England, the Whigs and the Tories, clearly diſtinguiſh the difference of their principles. The latter, eager and violent in the profecution of their objects, conſtantly preſerve themſelves in a cloſe and compact body, ready for action. The Whigs, mild in diſpoſition, and wary in their purſuits, are looſe and unconnected, and require a long time to be ſet in motion. The principles of the Tories, leading them to the ſupport of a very high prerogative, approaching in many points nearly to abſolute power, render them ſubmiſſive to authority, always prepared to obey their leaders, and ſeldom queſtioning the lawfulneſs of their commands.

The Whigs, who are attached to a monarchy, secured by limits, which they conceive it more necessary to contract than to extend, are tenacious of their privileges, and must be convinced of the rectitude of a measure before they can be brought to support it. When the parties come into action, they shew the same difference of conduct as appears between bold confidence and reflective courage. The one, hasty and impetuous; the other, cautious and temperate. The consequences of victory have been equally shewn both in the forbearance and moderation of the Whigs, and in the insolent and vindictive triumphs of the Tories.

I have been thus particular in these distinctions of character, as a late great event in England, the dissolution of Parliament, has strongly marked them.

The Tories maintain the measure upon principle. The chief men amongst them, who were formerly zealously attached to the

the Stuart race, conceive that the present King is entitled to their support; yet the two first kings of his family, who governed upon Whig principles, met with opposition from their party.

Whigs, in general, have not the good sense to make this distinction. Many of them, from long habits of attachment to the house of Brunswick, direct their views to the family of the prince, and not to the principles upon which his ministers (for he can do no wrong) may govern. But the conduct of the far greater part of them, especially the Dissenters, arises from their disgust to the principal Whig families who formed the coalition with Lord North. By thus sacrificing their principles to their resentment, they involve themselves in the same ruin which they have brought upon their leaders. Whether they were justified or not for the part which they have taken is not now (though it shall be hereafter) a matter of consideration. The fact is, that the Whigs have

have joined an administration in support of the extension of the prerogative beyond a certain boundary, and have censured the representatives of the people for attempting to restrain it.

This gross misconduct of the Whigs has contributed much more to the destruction of their party than the artifices which have been practised, and the attacks which have been made upon them, by their avowed enemies, during a series of much more than twenty years. They have suffered by delusion — they have laboured under oppression; yet when they have been roused to the exertion of their strength, they have proved formidable opponents. But now their whole consequence is departed; and Tory ministers, having gained their point in dividing them, no longer apprehend even the semblance of opposition.

It has been generally observed, that striking expressions, industriously spread amongst

amongst the people, have produced the most instantaneous and sudden effects. The words " number forty-five" made the fortune of John Wilkes. The words " Coalition, and taking away of chartered " rights," ruined the Whig leaders. The taking away these very chartered rights at several periods since the year 1773, produced neither complaint nor murmur: yet by the good management of those who *presumed* to call themselves the King's friends, in diligently distributing an immense number of pamphlets and newspapers through every even the most remote parts of the kingdom, the India Bill of Mr. Fox was rendered one of the most unpopular measures that has been known in England since the famous Jew Bill. This was the trumpet which sounded the destruction of the Portland Administration. It is the sound, not the meaning of words, which prevail amidst popular clamours.

I shall not take up much of your time in comments upon this memorable bill. The

The subject is almost worn out. I shall barely mention the leading features of the two bills of Mr. Fox and Mr. Pitt. The first of them vested the principal appointments in Parliament, divesting the Crown of any immediate control over them. This disposition, agreeable to the spirit of a Whig government, and for which there were many precedents,- was yet severely condemned by the body of the Whigs. The bill of Mr. Pitt vested these appointments in, and under the control of, the Crown. This was agreeable to the spirit of his administration, which is carried on upon Tory principles. But the Tories had not the folly of the Whigs. Steady to their principles, they supported and applauded the measure.

The other parts of the two bills, which relate to the direction of the affairs of the Company, differ very little in essential matters. They equally take away the monopolizing chartered rights, which was charged to the late Administration as an enormous

enormous crime. The Company ought to have been diffolved long ago. It is worthy of our attention, that every European affociation for the Eaft-India trade has become infolvent. The Dutch Eaft-India Company, hitherto the moſt flouriſhing in Europe, is in a miferable condition. The affairs of all the companies have been firſt difordered by an unprofitable trade. The depravity of their fervants has completed their ruin. It would have been for the interefts of this country as well as thofe of humanity, that this trade had been long ago fuppreffed. The nation had been fooner freed from a heavy burden, and the wretched inhabitants of India delivered from the deftructive pangs of mercilefs plunderers. The Mahomedan conquerors robbed thefe poor people only of the fleece. The Chriſtian traders deprive them both of fleece and fkins.

But what muft be the principles of thofe Whigs, who, having deſtroyed the power of the firſt Whig families in the country,

regarded,

regarded, without oppofition or complaint, a ftroke levelled at the root of the deareft privileges of Englifhmen, depriving them of the right of trial by jury? In the laft India Bill has been fubftituted another jurifdiction, a Court of Star Chamber, (fo far as it extends) in the place of the common courts of juftice. It is no excufe to fay that the peculiar fituation of the criminals made a new fpecies of jurifdiction neceffary. We have already courts of juftice independent of the Crown. If thefe will not perform their duty, can the execution of it be expected from that Eaft-India court of judicature in which the Crown muft neceffarily have an influence? Juries are feldom deficient in their duty. The jury found the culprits of the Madras government guilty: but what was the fentence paffed by the Court?—I fhall apply this fubject to another part of this work.

I fhall fay a few words upon the famous coalition, though it muft be with caution; for

for there appears so many solid arguments on both sides of the question, and the abilities and the integrity of the principal Whig leaders who coalesced with Lord North are so fully established, that, although I am one of those who very sincerely wish that the coalition had never taken place, I should think myself highly culpable in forming any opinion of censure. I look upon either the Duke of Portland, the Cavendishes, or Lord Fitzwilliam, in this case, as I would upon Cato, when he was found early in the morning in the streets of Rome. If they were in an error, it was an error of virtue.

I must first premise, that I have not the smallest design of exculpating Lord North from any part of his administration. God forbid that I should be the defender of a man, who, if not the principal, was one of the instruments made use of in carrying on the most abandoned measures of the new system, especially in conducting the reproachful part of that system, the

fatal

fatal war waged againſt our American fellow ſubjects.

But whilſt I thus ſeverely tax this nobleman with crimes of an enormous magnitude, I ought to do him the juſtice to ſay, that, having refuſed, unmoved even by prayers or reproaches, requeſts from a moſt powerful quarter, either to accept the Treaſury or to form an adminiſtration himſelf, he threw himſelf wholly upon the mercy of the Whigs, ſubmitting himſelf to be diſpoſed of at their pleaſure. He offered either to remain in, or to retire wholly from, any adminiſtration which might be formed.

This is, indeed, a ſmall recompence for the miſchiefs which he has cauſed; but as there can be no reaſon to doubt his ſincerity in this inſtance, he deſerves ſome credit, at leaſt from the Whigs, for his conduct.

I am

I am sensible that it is no argument in favour of the late coalition to assert, that the present Administration is equally liable to the same objections: but it is but fair to state both sides of a question. It is a fact that, in every measure, of which Lord North was nominally the head, three very distinguished members, now acting under the present ministry, had, at least, an equal participation; perhaps, from their greater activity, a larger share. Mr. Jenkinson, Mr. Robinson, and Mr. Atkinson, so much the objects of popular censure, and nearly the whole of the former supporters of Lord North's administration, are now strenuous in support of the present minister, Mr. Pitt. In respect to the coalition, therefore, the Whigs, who, upon the principle of condemning their leaders for the coalition with Lord North, support the coalition of Mr. Pitt with such men, are acting a very criminal part.

I have said that I am one of those who most heartily wish that the coalition with Lord

Lord North had never taken place. No good has arisen from it; and eventually much mischief. It was not a desirable union. Men of the highest honour and integrity were linked with characters whose conduct they had frequently and justly condemned. It was well enough said*, *Amicitias immortales inimicitias mortales esse debere.* I shall make this addition to the historian — If it is the duty of a Christian to forgive, it is not a part of his duty to take to his bosom the men whose actions he had so justly condemned.

The situation of the principal Whig families, the remaining party of Lord Rockingham, at the time when they submitted to enter into this coalition, ought to be taken into consideration. Their families, which had been long at the head of the Whigs, were now become little more than the shadow of that formidable phalanx which had driven out not only the osten-

---

* Our enmities ought to be mortal, our friendships eternal.

sible administration of Lord North, but the secret junto, whose power had been too banefully predominant. They had this alternative — to retire wholly from public life, and give up the contest for ever, or to make use of the party influence of a man whose principles they disliked, and whose measures they had constantly opposed. They made choice of the latter.

It was a tempting offer. They had the experience of past ages to support the opinion, that a majority of the House of Commons constituted the strength of administration: and they were sensible that by making use of the parliamentary influence of Lord North and his friends, they should have an opportunity, the only one perhaps that would present itself, of establishing a government upon Whig principles.

In the forming of that administration, the Whig leaders cannot be charged with having

having acted from interested or pecuniary views. In the disposal of places, the far greater part of them were given to those with whom they had coalesced. The hackneyed reports of the emoluments which the minister secured to his family was a shameful abuse of the public. A poor solitary place, of about 500l. per annum, given to the minister's brother, constitutes the mighty fruits which his family enjoy from his administration; and even this very place was pressed upon him in a most honourable manner from a most exalted quarter, after the minister had made a different disposition of it.

How far it is, in a strict sense, lawful for a virtuous man to join with those of whose principles he has a bad opinion, in endeavours to bring about purposes of good, is a question, which, in the present corrupt state of Great Britain, I shall not take upon me to determine. In such an instance, however, I need not hesitate to say, that a conduct, founded upon good motives,

motives, merits commendation much more than it admits reproof.

I am sure I need not scruple confidently to assert, that the good of their fellow subjects was alone the motive which induced either Lord Rockingham or the Duke of Portland to accept the administration. It was a sacrifice to patriotism, which cost the much-lamented Marquis his life; and it was owing to a serenity of temper, which marks one of the most spotless characters of this or any age, that the Duke of Portland was preserved from the ill consequences of incessant vexation and fatigue.

I am myself one of those old-fashioned Whigs who pay a respect to character and connection. So long as I saw a Cavendish, a Bentinck, or a Fitzwilliam, remnants of the party of the honoured name of Rockingham, acting upon the hereditary principles of their ancestors, I should think it my duty to support them; and I also

also think that sober men would do the same.

There was one neglected measure during their administration, the settlement of the American commerce, which has made some of the Whigs suspect that the influence of Lord North and his friends was by far too powerful in the Cabinet. The proclamation, shutting out the Americans from the West-India ports, has been given in proof of this assertion. This affair wants elucidation. I shall attempt it in a letter dedicated merely to the explanations of some motions in the machine of government, which are not generally known to the public. It will appear as a paradox to say that the Whig leaders might have settled the American treaty satisfactorily to their own principles, although they themselves conceived that they had not the power to do it: but this was the case, and shall be hereafter explained.

Such is the ſtate of our Government, with little hope of its either receiving the juſt and proper tone of a Whig adminiſtration, or of being ever eſtabliſhed upon a ſettled or permanent foundation; at leaſt, without ſome great convulſion, the conſequence of which muſt be both expected and dreaded. — Farewel.

From on board the Britannia, at ſea, Oct. 26, 1784.

LETTER VI.

EXPLANATION

OF THE

APPARENT CONTRADICTION

IN THE

ACTIONS OF THE PRINCIPAL WHIG LEADERS

WITH RESPECT TO AMERICA,

AT TWO DIFFERENT PERIODS OF TIME.

LETTER. VI.

TO ⎯⎯⎯⎯

THE subject upon which I am about to enter is very difficult to explain. Those who live within the circle of the Court are alone competent to the comprehension of the motives which govern the actions of ministers. The intrigues of the closet in a free country, where the ministers frequently act independently of the Crown, are a labyrinth difficult to be explored. We are, therefore, not to be surprised at the imperfect and fallacious accounts which are continually transmitted to the world by pretenders to this kind of knowledge; or at either the credulity or incredulity (for they have each their effects upon men of different dispositions) which narratives of the intrigues of a Court produce. The manners of a Court being chiefly confined to its circle, the persons within it live very much amongst themselves. A knowledge, therefore, of what passes in the Court generally centers within its own bounds.

In treating upon this subject, great delicacy is required. Much mischief may accrue from injudicious information. It would prove of no utility to the public, and might involve private persons in many difficulties. No other purpose could be answered by it than that of gratifying an idle curiosity. There is equally a general law of propriety, as there is a general law of nations, which must influence every man of justness of thinking, even though the narrator has entirely quitted the scene of action.

A great part of the respect which is paid to statesmen is owing to the density of the veil which covers their actions. The people are lost in the obscurity in which these affairs

affairs are involved, and adore the invifibility of thofe, who, like an eaftern monarch, perform them behind the curtain of ftate. Should this veil be withdrawn, they would behold activity and indolence, fenfe and weaknefs, diligence and diffipation, mingled together in the character of a ftatefman, much in the fame manner as amongft themfelves.

What I chiefly promifed was to explain the apparent contradiction in the actions of the principal Whig leaders, with refpect to America, at the two following periods of time:—The firft of thefe periods was when Lord Rockingham came into office in April, 1782. That excellent nobleman refufed to accept the adminiftration until the conditions which he ftipulated to be performed were previoufly agreed to by the Court. One of thofe ftipulations was, that an immediate end fhould be put to the American war, and the independence of the United States unconditionally granted. The laft of thefe periods

periods was when the Duke of Portland came into administration in conjunction with Lord North, Lord Stormont, and Lord Carlisle; men who had hitherto acted upon opposite principles to him.

The Whig party amongst the people ascribed to the influence of these three noblemen in the Cabinet the apparent neglect of every measure that had a tendency to conciliate the affections of America; and that it was wholly owing to this circumstance that neither minister nor consul were appointed to the United States.

To the same cause they also ascribed the establishment of that adverse regulation, preventing the Americans from entering into the West-India ports. In short, they attributed to their influence an apparent want of inclination to enter into any connections whatsoever with the United States.

These

These apprehensions, however, (so far as I have been able to learn) were founded only in part, and related merely to the prohibitory parts of the former commercial intercourse between Great Britain, her remaining colonies, and the United States. The advice of persons, highly prejudiced against those states, and who took a very strong part in the war, had certainly the preference. The advice of one person in particular, who has long occupied a second department in the State, and who was active in the promotion of the American war, bore a great sway with a minister of the first abilities. The assiduity of that person is great, and he is generally supposed to be a tolerable master of commercial subjects.

These qualities, it must be supposed, recommended him to this minister. It would have been a fortunate circumstance had his occupations suffered him, and surely this was one of the most important affairs of state, to have taken the trouble of of thinking, upon this occafion, for him-felf. Had he admitted the fubject into his own confideration, he would have perceived, that if thefe meafures (as they were probably defigned) wounded America, they wounded much more deeply his own country. Though he might not be fo converfant in commercial affairs himfelf, his amazingly quick and comprehenfive conception would have foon fupplied every deficiency.

But, to take up this meafure upon another ground, if he confidered the proclamation (as it was ftated by another high authority, whofe veracity is not to be called in queftion) to be merely temporary till the treaty was regulated, why was it continued after every idea of a commercial treaty was given up? There is a fubtilty in fome of our modern politicians which often holds out fome fpecious regulation (whether commercial or otherwife) for the fake of gaining popularity; but fuch delufions coft a nation very dear, when,

when, as in this case, they are purchased with great and decisive advantages. I must not, however, impute such delusory schemes to this minister. He has more manliness of temper, and is much more disposed to set popularity at defiance. His conduct, therefore, could not have arisen from this cause.

That the advice to which I have referred should be taken by this minister, in preference, has produced much speculation. There was another man, equally (I shall not be thought to do injustice to the person whom I have alluded to, if I say more) able and intelligent, to whom the application would have been made with much greater propriety. The extent of his knowledge, the consistency of his conduct, and the integrity of his principles, pointed him out as less likely to act from passion or prejudice. This character survives, and I hope will long survive, for the benefit of that country which has the honour to call him her subject. His own country

country has proved ungrateful to deserving merit. She is not worthy of him. It remains to conjecture why such an application was not made.

The following observation, founded on experience, may possibly assist our conjectures:—that the greater the abilities of any man, if he has not birth or fortune to support them, the greater is the jealousy which they excite, and the stronger are the attempts to depress them.

Should even his tenacious integrity, extending to the most rigorous sense of justice and propriety, be proof against every means of advancing his fortune, it will not procure him the thanks, much less the praise, of this degenerate age. Birth or fortune will alone enable such a man to silence jealousy, and to command attention.

This is a digression, which, indeed, this letter will in a great measure be. I shall, however, now come to the principal point —a dif-

—a discussion of the question, whether the late Administration was more inclined to enter into a friendly connection with the United States, or to deal hostilely with them? I am convinced myself of the disposition of the principal Whig leaders in the administration to have entered into a mutually beneficial treaty with America; and I consider the following circumstance to be the cause of this disposition not being carried into execution:—When the ministers tried the ground in one of the highest quarters, where they were indispensably obliged to mention the measures which they designed to pursue, they met with so cold a reception, that they judged it most conducive to the safety of their administration to defer their intended purposes.

It is very probable that some of their colleagues might be forward in magnifying the danger of pressing a measure, which they represented as a very delicate point to discuss in the presence of a higher power.

They might also be privately gratified with the effects which had been produced, as they proved a bar to any conciliatory measures being entered into with America. This, however, is only a conjecture formed upon their general conduct; for I have been informed, from the best authority, that they never made any opposition, or gave the least obstruction to the proposal of the measure.

I am well assured that I am very correct in these circumstances. I know that I am equally so in the assertion, that the Whig leaders were mistaken in the judgement which they formed upon this occasion. Their cool reception arose less from disinclination to enter into a treaty with America, than from a general dislike of their administration.

They certainly tried a much more delicate point in the bill for the regulation of the affairs of the East-India Company. An examination into these affairs by independent

pendent parliamentary commiſſioners, was very ill calculated, for many weighty private reaſons, to meet approbation in the cloſet. This was a *ſanctum ſanctorum*, which the Court would have riſqued its exiſtence rather than ſuffer any other commiſſioners than of its own appointment to have entered.

They did not diſtinguiſh with their uſual ability between the difference of the reception which they met with on theſe two meaſures. They were not ſaluted by a cold reception when they made the application upon this ſubject; nor had they reaſon to ſuppoſe, from appearances, that their bill gave the leaſt diſguſt; yet the conſequence of that bill was a clap of thunder, which burſt upon them in an inſtant, and cruſhed them to atoms.

The Whigs had been long habituated to labour in the ſchool of oppoſition: for more than twenty years they had only two ſmall intervals. The firſt adminiſtration

tion of Lord Rockingham lafted twelve months: it fupported itfelf through one feffion of Parliament againft the whole force of the Court, all the houfehold fervants voting againft that minifter. What was attempted in vain by force, was very foon after effected by intrigue. The fecond adminiftration of that nobleman ended, with his life, in three months: but intrigues to deftroy this adminiftration were carried on even during that fhort period, chiefly by one of that Cabinet. Both thefe adminiftrations, equally with their own, were formed contrary to fome *particular* inclination, and they met with the fame fate.

The period of the laft adminiftration was very near drawing to a clofe within three months after their appointment, when the fettlement of the Prince of Wales's houfehold was in agitation. The manner in which that affair had been conducted, at leaft as far as a comparifon can be formed between the Court and Parliament, me n tre fembled, in many of its parts, the India Bill, and, had the intrigues of the Court been ripe, would have produced the fame confequences. The train was laid, and Mr. Pitt was at hand: but, in the moment of execution, the Court, on fecond confideration, did not think proper to fet fire to it. Perhaps they imagined the ground of difmiffion not to be fufficiently ftrong to expect the fupport neceffary to an adminiftration of their own. Had they been prepared, the fubmiffion of the minifters would not have faved them. This commotion, therefore, as it began with threats, ended with careffes.

They underftood thefe careffes too well to be wholly deceived by them; yet they were not without fome effect; by fetting them off their guard, other motives influenced their conduct. They had been recommended to avoid all manner of difference in a certain quarter, as the only means of preferving their adminiftration. Some of their coadjutors had been educated in thefe principles, and were eager to promote them. The Whig leaders followed this fatal advice, and, in a moment, cancelled the falutary effects of an experience which had been the work of their lives.

I am fatisfied that the motives of the Whig families were good, and that the bad effects which this conduct, in fome very principal perfons amongft them, produced, were owing to the exercife of an amiable human weaknefs. There are few men, I fpeak from many years attentive obfervation, who have a more clear and enlightened judgement — there is no man who has a greater chaftity of manners, or a more unfhaken integrity, than the late firft minifter; yet thefe great qualities were rendered of lefs effect to the public by a diffidence of his own abilities. This amiable weaknefs made him, on this occafion, acquiefce in opinions that were calculated for an artificial, not for his manly character. Had this excellent perfon fortunately purfued his own mature judgement,

judgement, an immediate and lasting connection would have been formed with the United States of America. He would have found no opposition, had he persisted in his intentions. The mind of one in power to dictate was fully made up to the measure.

It is the especial duty of ministers, acting upon Whig principles, in this limited monarchy, and who are responsible, not so much to the sovereign as to the people, *respectfully* to address a king with truth, simplicity, and firmness. Had the late ministers performed this duty, they would have acquired strength in that quarter which they were accustomed to approach with apprehension.

Besides, they risqued nothing by a resolute and manly conduct. They knew what compulsively occasioned the surrender of the administration into their hands. They had improvidently left the whole body of household troops secure in office;

yet these, they were assured, would act in opposition, the moment they received their orders from a junto. It was only an additional instance to their former experience, that when the signal was thrown out for battle, they instantly obeyed, and gave the ministers a decisive defeat. No sooner were some particular intentions, with respect to the India Bill, discovered by Lords of the Bedchamber, and other Lords of the Household, who had left their proxies with the ministers to vote for the bill, than they instantly withdrew them, and voted against it. They had, therefore, no medium of conciliation to trust to. It was of course immaterial whether any measures of their proposal met with a cool or a courteous reception. The former, perhaps, was the most agreeable, as it would have been the most sincere. Neither opportunity nor inclination was wanting to decide their fate.

Such is the ascendency of virtue, that the principal men of the Whig party met
with

with respect even from the throne; yet not as ministers, but as subjects. It is plain that, by this mode of reasoning, I do not speak of the perfections, but of the infirmities of mankind. The passions of persons of the *most-exalted* rank are, at the best, like those of other men; generally speaking, they are much worse.—I shall defer the conclusion of this subject to my next letter. I must now bid you farewel.

From on board the Britannia, at sea,
    October 27, 1784.

LETTER

LETTER VII.

THE SAME SUBJECT CONTINUED.

Stat sua cuique dies; breve et irreparabile tempus
Omnibus est vitæ; sed famam extendere factis,
Hoc virtutis opus.
                                        VIRG.

LETTER VII.

TO ⸺⸺⸺⸺

IN all affairs which have borne any relation to America, whether before or since the independence of that country, a fatality seems to have prevailed in our councils. The former measures of Government, carried on upon system amidst the highest departments, and supported by the far greater part of the people, were pursued with such obduracy and perverseness, as to preclude all consideration of the ruin into which they were themselves actually plunging. When some of the people recovered from their delusion sufficiently to enable the better part of the Whigs to exert their whole strength, an end was put to this wretched system of government, and the acceptance of a Whig administration

tion became almoſt a matter of compulſion: yet this was no ſooner obtained, than new difficulties aroſe to prevent the ſucceſs of their meaſures.

Many circumſtances in the ſtate of our national affairs concurred to favour Lord Rockingham at his entrance into the adminiſtration. He was at the head of a great and powerful party, attached to him by the moſt honourable motives, an affectionate reſpect for his perſon, and a confident ſecurity in his principles. His parts were ſtrong and uſeful; his judgement ſolid and mature; his temper calm and unruffled. All his meaſures were taken with extreme caution; but when he had decided, his reſolution was fixed and unſhaken. The conſtant ſerenity of his mind protected him againſt the effects of fortune. Proſperity never begetting in him unreaſonable deſires; adverſity always giving ſtrength to his natural firmneſs.

He

He was educated in the Court of King George the Second, and imbibed an early attachment to the principles of his government, which he practised with a zeal that bordered upon enthusiasm. This appeared, though without the least bigotry, in the most trifling incidents. His natural disposition would have led him to prefer private to public life. After his first administration, in which he conducted himself with vigour and ability, he was very averse to take upon him the government. He expressed a desire to have his part in the administration confined to a seat in the Cabinet; but such was the situation of our affairs, and such the implicit and unbounded confidence which the public placed in his integrity, (in this opinion there was no distinction of party) that it was become a matter of necessity for him to assume the administration.

I am not one of those who are fond of expatiating on the independence of public upon private virtue. I shall, therefore, mention,

mention, though it is not necessary to my subject, the private virtues of this great character; in which the excellencies of each were strikingly conspicuous. I think myself fully justified in this digression, since I present an illustrious example worthy of all imitation.

Of the first nobility, and inheriting an immense paternal estate, he so happily blended affability of temper with dignity of manners, and magnificence of spirit with generous hospitality, that he became equally the object of affection and reverence. Few possessed a more happy talent of reconciling differences amongst men, or of putting an end to the dissentions of parties. His patience and forbearance removing the grounds of dispute; the affectionate mildness of his disposition inclining even inveterate enemies to reconciliation.

He possessed an unaffected piety, without any mixture of sourness or ostentation;

was regular in his devotions, both at church and in his own chapel, where service was regularly performed. He was always greatly attached to domestic life; and, in a long and happy connection with his excellent Lady, afforded, in his high station, a very striking and eminent example. His doors were constantly open: his mornings and evenings regularly spent in the reception of his friends: his ample table was filled with guests; and, in his absence from the country, a table was regularly kept for the accommodation of any gentleman whom pleasure or business led to his house.

He was fond of agriculture, and spent a very great part of his large income in improvements. His principal residence in the country was equally distinguished for its elegance and grandeur, its usefulness and hospitality: it was laid out upon a great and extensive plan, and contained within its bounds an immense pile of building. He cultivated a great part of his estate himself; was perfectly well acquainted with its various distribution, and consumed the produce within the house. He had artificers of all kinds, who received their daily food within the walls, and for whom he erected shops and houses to live in, all within the circle of the offices. The lively appearance of the country about him, in which were to be seen variety of works carrying on, mines sinking for coal, canals digging for its conveyance, experiments in husbandry and gardening, and elegant buildings arising to beautify the estate, all in one view, served to display the taste and splendour, the wisdom and beneficence of the sensible and magnificent owner. Happily for his country, the heir to his estate is also an heir to his virtues.

I leave a subject which always calls for the deepest and most sincere regret. The unequivocal proofs of friendship and regard which I received from this excellent person will for ever engage me to pay to his

his revered memory the grateful tribute of affectionate remembrance.—I now return to a more unpleasant work.

No sooner had the Whigs completed the destruction of the administration of Lord North, and of the wretched system upon which he was employed, than, all farther resistance appearing vain, the Chancellor was sent to Lord Rockingham, desiring him to form an administration. That nobleman expressed his wishes that the measures of government, upon which the future administration was to be carried on, should be previously settled. This, on the part of the Chancellor, was strongly combated: but Lord Rockingham, having a very full experience of the general conduct of the Court party, and being sensible that they meant to avoid all those measures which the Whigs had been strenuous in supporting, firmly refused to take any step till the whole was arranged.

For some days, to the great surprise of every one, neither message nor answer was sent. At length, Lord S. waited upon Lord Rockingham, and made him acquainted that he had received instructions to co-operate with him in settling an administration. The Court, not being able to shake the resolution of Lord Rockingham, had sent for Lord S. knowing his disposition to be favourable to their purposes.

It is the etiquette of the Court, whenever a person is desired to form an administration, to consider him at the head of it: at least, this was the custom in better times, and was yet practised, when a necessity arose for forming a Whig administration. Lord S. was, therefore, properly speaking, the Court minister.

At this meeting Lord S. urged Lord Rockingham to enter upon the business of forming the administration, leaving the measures to be pursued for farther discussion;

sion; but the noble Marquis not only refused him this request, but even to enter into any kind of negociation whatever through his medium.

Lord Rockingham was for a long time clear and decided in this resolution, and declared openly his marked disapprobation. The negociation hung in suspence till, at length, the principal Whigs, thinking that the risque of its being broken off was greater than the trusting it to Lord S., were earnest in entreating him to recede from his opinion. Their request was not, however, immediately complied with. He repeatedly warned them against the ill consequence of submitting. At length, wearied out with their importunities, and, contrary to his better judgement, he consented, at their intreaty, to meet Lord S.

But although he gave up to his friends the resolution which he had made not to enter into a negociation through the medium of Lord S., he inflexibly adhered to that

that which demanded a previous settlement of all the public measures to be carried on by the administration which he was desired to form. He made Lord S. acquainted with these proposed measures when they met. The latter readily gave up the naming of the administration; but appeared desirous of evading any discussion concerning measures: the meeting, therefore, was without effect.

At length, the House of Commons becoming uneasy at having no Administration, a full meeting of the Whig members of both Houses were convened at Lord Rockingham's. This meeting, having approved his conduct, and given him the strongest assurances of their support, prepared a motion for the next day in the House of Commons, which they directed to be communicated to Lord S.

This decided measure produced an immediate effect. When the House met, it was informed that a message had been sent

to

to Lord Rockingham to acquaint him that his propofals were fully agreed to. The Adminiftration was then formed; in the arrangement of which he confulted the mildnefs and benignity of his difpofition, including, in the Cabinet, all the principal members of oppofition, without exception *; perhaps with too much eafe; certainly in the provifion which was demanded for the two friends of Lord S.; Mr. Dunning and Colonel Barré. But Lord S. having the actual power at Court, and a much more important meafure being given up to him, (even the Chancellor being fuffered to remain) it was not thought prudent to refufe this demand.

---

* Lord Rockingham,
  Lord Keppel,
  Lord John Cavendifh, ⎫
  Duke of Richmond,   ⎬ Friends of Lord Rockingham.
  Mr. Fox,   ⎭
  Lord S.
  Mr. Dunning, friend to Lord S.
  Lord Camden, generally acts with Lord S.
  Duke of Grafton,   ⎫
  General Conway,   ⎬ of no particular party.
  Lord Thurlow, of Lord North's adminiftration.

When the whole arrangement was made, the King faw Lord Rockingham.

The putting an immediate end to the American war, and an unconditional acknowledgement of the independence of the United States of America, was, as I have already mentioned, one of the meafures which Lord Rockingham infifted upon, and which were agreed to by the Court. The others do not regard this fubject.

The prediction of the noble Marquis was verified almoft the inftant Lord S. took his feat in the Cabinet. His conftitution was delicate, incapable of fupporting him in a conteft full of vexation. A violent illnefs enfued, from which he recovered in fome meafure; but this was but a gleam of fhort continuance.

Lord S. purfued his inftructions with fpirit and diligence. He knew that the American queftions afforded the moft probable

bable ground for perplexing the councils of the new ministers; some of whom were very lukewarm in their sentiments. The C., who had been suffered to remain in place, was certainly not the warmest of the advocates in favour of America, and Mr. Dunning was professedly devoted to Lord S.: his ground, therefore, was strong. He offered a preamble to a bill which he was bringing into the House, that involved all the points in dispute respecting America; and he made such objections to the independence of that country, which was expressly agreed upon to be unconditionally granted, as effectually to delay its execution.

Had Lord Rockingham recovered from his illness, it is probable that he would have obliged Lord S. either to alter his conduct, or to retire from administration. The dread which the Court party had of his power, and the confidence which the nation placed in him, combining with the general opinion, at that time, of the necessity

sity of the Administration being entrusted to his care, warrant the conjecture.

When his illness obliged him to retire from business, the field was left open to Lord S. Mr. Fox, with whom rested the execution of the measures respecting the independence of America, which were then under the consideration of the Cabinet Council, found himself in a minority, and therefore incapable of obtaining its grant in that unconditional manner, which had been previously agreed upon: he therefore thought it necessary, first consulting the situation of Lord Rockingham, who then lay in a very doubtful state, to resign his office.

This was soon determined by the decease of that amiable and valuable person. It was decreed by Providence that this nation should be humbled in the dust. The general grief was sincere and unaffected.

The loss of this excellent person proved an accession of great strength to the Court party. Lord S. succeeded, in course, as first minister. He began early with the discussion of the American question, and made a vehement protestation, that the moment the independence of America should become granted, the sun of Great Britain must set for ever.

When Lord S. became the minister, he, doubtless, found reason to suppose that opinions in a certain quarter were not averse even to granting independence to America. A discovery, which he might well consider as the utmost consequence to the duration of his power, as it facilitated the making peace, which he considered to be the foundation of a long administration to himself.

There is no judgement to be formed of the account which Lord S. gave in Parliament of the provisional treaty. I am well assured that it proceeded more from the habit,

habit, to which he had been long accuſtomed, of giving indirect explanations: but, it had the effect of making people at that time believe there was ſome myſtery concealed under the treaty. — My next letter will conclude this part of my ſubject. — Farewel.

From on board the Britannia, at ſea,
    Oct. 29, 1784.

LETTER

LETTER VIII.

ON THE
NECESSITY
OF VESTING THE
ADMINISTRATION OF GOVERNMENT
IN AN
ABLE AND VIGOROUS MINISTER.

Præclara igitur conscientia sustentor, cum cogito me de republica: aut meruisse optime cum potuerim: aut certe nunquam, nisi diviné, cogitasse: eaque ipsa tempestate reversam esse rempublicam, quam ego quatuor decem annis ante prospexerim.

CIC. ad ATT.

C OULD we suppose a prince in the situation of having committed faults, it might follow that he would find a full remedy in expiation; and this by throwing himself into the hands of those, but those only, who had been the tried friends of his family. This country can boast a subject whose character is exactly adapted to take the lead in administration, even during the most distracted state of affairs. The following lines of Horace will confirm much more than any thing that I can say, the lofty constancy of this person's mind in the most arduous trials:

Justum

* *Justum et tenacem propositi virum,*
   Non civium ardor prava jubentium,
Non vultus instantis tyranni
   Mente quatit solida, neque auster,
Dux inquieti turbidus Adriæ,
Nec fulminantis magna Jovis manus:
Si fractus illabatur orbis,
Impavidum ferient ruinæ.

His abilities are, beyond any comparison, the first in the present age. His knowledge so comprehensive and profound, as scarcely to find an equal even in the different learned professions, which require a life of study. He has a force of eloquence, which, for the combined powers

---

* The man in conscious virtue bold,
   Who dares his secret purpose hold,
Unshaken hears the crowd's tumultuous cries,
And the impetuous tyrant's angry brow defies.
   Let the wild winds that rule the seas,
   Tempestuous all their horrors raise;
Let Jove's dread arm with thunders rend the spheres,
Beneath the crush of worlds undaunted he appears.
                              Francis's Horace.

of brilliancy, fire, imagination, strength and fluency of ideas, excels the best speakers of modern times; perhaps rivals the first orators of antiquity.

These astonishing talents are supported by a vigour and activity of mind, which is perpetually employed in some useful plans of government. Had such powers been called into action when the nation was in prosperity, they would have been the means of supporting its grandeur. Were they called into action now, they would be the means (as far as human power can avail) of preserving it from ruin.

But it is one of those paradoxes, for which this age is famous, that every one confesses the greatness of his parts, and has a thorough conviction of his integrity, yet no one follows his advice: and thus is a life of above fifty years, matured by experience amidst severe trials, and grown gray in the service of the public, suffered to fall a sacrifice to the poignant feelings of his own mind, brooding over the disordered situation of his private affairs, of which his attention to the public has been the cause; yet still wholly engrossed by that very public which has proved itself undeserving of him.

The extraordinary abilities which he possesses neither render his manners harsh nor assuming, nor derogate in the least degree from the character of the agreeable companion, the soothing and affectionate friend. He is a domestic man, intimately connected with, and attached to, his family. Liberal and indulgent in his construction of the actions of others, he is rigorous and severe in the construction of his own. His integrity has been put to the proof. He has rejected the means of advancing his fortune by methods which many men of the fairest characters would not have scrupled to use, that certainly would not have been of the smallest injury to to the public, and yet have proved of material service to a worthy individual.

He has his failings: at least, if I may hazard this term, so infinitely superior are those virtues by which they are obscured; but if they must have that appellation given to them, they are no more than the imperfections of a great and generous mind. In the opinion of some of his friends, he is too indiscriminate in his praise, has great warmth of temper, and an aptitude to enforce his measures with too much heat and perseverance.

If, in attempts to gain any accession of strength to his party, to defend some unfortunate person, or to establish a man in his principles by well-timed applause, he sometimes exceeds the strict bounds to which he limits himself on the more important measures of government, they are wholly excited by a benevolent disposition, always exerted on these occasions with force, and generally with affection.

In this particular quality he bears a striking resemblance to Cicero. The praises of both, though influenced by the best motives, appear too indiscriminate, and destroy the effect which the applause of such excellent judges would otherwise produce. We are struck with the brilliancy and fire of their eloquence, and often return to the orator those very praises which were meant by him as the reward of modest merit, which is thus deprived of that elation of mind which the chastity of their praise would otherwise effect. In the greatness of their parts, and their general pursuits, these illustrious statesmen have also a strong similitude. In their disposition, however, they widely differ. The characteristic of the person of whom we speak is firmness and decision, wholly opposite both to the vanity and despondence of mind which forms so prevalent a part in the character of the noble Roman.

But

But may I aſk theſe queſtions?—Ought not ſome allowance to be made for the want of temper in a man of theſe high qualities, who finds himſelf neglected not only by the public, in whoſe ſervice he has been long toiling, but by even his own friends? Again, how long do theſe ſudden marks of diſguſt to his friends (they will not bear the name of reſentment) continue? And what has been the return that he has made to a neglect which (I am not ſingle in opinion) proceeds, in ſome of them at leaſt, from jealouſy of his great parts?

I have deſired the liberty of aſking theſe queſtions for the ſake of explaining the nature of the complaints which are made of this excellent perſon; and I hope to be indulged with that of anſwering them. The warmth of temper ſhewn by him in public aſſemblies may be eſteemed by cautious men a want of prudence: but as we may apply the words which Cornelius Nepos uſes, when he ſpeaks of Cicero, to this

this person, "*Non enim Cicero ea solum quæ vivo se acciderant futura prædixit, sed etiam quæ nunc usu veniunt, cecinit ut vates,"* we should be careful how far, under this conviction of mind, we ought to censure a conduct which arises from strong feelings, from a consciousness of rectitude, and from an urgency of desire to promote the public welfare.

It is unnecessary to say much upon the warmth of temper, the sudden impulses of passion, which he has sometimes shewn when he has differed in opinion from his friends. These have, in general, been little more than a temporary disgust at such of their actions as were irreconcilable to his own judgement, and never extended beyond wishes to retire from attendance on measures which did not meet with his approbation.

* For Cicero not only pointed out the events which came to pass in his own life, but he predicted, as a prophet, even those that were brought about in our days.

If we, however, confider this matter more at large, and pay an attention to the behaviour of his friends to him, and his conduct in return, we fhall find that their inattention has been repaid merely by acts of friendfhip, and by public applaufe; fometimes, perhaps, too ftrongly marked. Whether he would have acted moft prudent in fubmitting wholly to the difpofition of his particular friends, or in taking independent ground of his own, is a queftion of fuch delicacy, that I cannot venture an opinion upon it.

He certainly, by taking a medium line of conduct, gave much uneafinefs to his friends. The motives on either fide were good; but they had not his force of mind. He was difturbed to fee thofe, to whom he had been long attached, and whofe fupport he fo ardently defired, averfe to the vigour of action which he was continually recommending to them. His friends, who, on their parts, notwithftanding thefe little differences, had a fincere affection for him, were, on the contrary, uneasy that he would not submit to their opinion.

These opinions he could not approve. His friends had submitted almost implicitly to some of their party, who, although in possession of the most shining talents, had neither those fixed principles, nor that regularity of conduct, requisite in the leader of a party acting upon principle. His own natural simplicity of disposition preserved him from any desire of rivalship, and his tenderness to his friends not only made him ultimately follow their example, but even take pains to shew that his friendship to the parties, whose conduct he thought most censurable, was not unimpaired.

Many struggles, however, consequently some warmth of temper, attended this compliance. From hence arose those complaints which some of his best friends made to one another, and to which I have been

been a frequent and painful confident. Those who were jealous of his parts endeavoured to improve these opportunities of lessening his influence; and they have had the effect of making his best friends, though not less warm in their regard for him, much more apprehensive of his temper. But in these complaints there was no consideration paid to the peculiarity of both their and his situation. They had involved themselves; he wished both to free himself and to set them free. The event has justified the propriety of his conduct; for it is an indisputable truth, that had his frequent admonitions been attended to by his friends, they would have been at this time a respectable, not a broken party.

My next and last consideration is, the imputation fixed upon him of an aptitude to enforce his measures with too much heat and perseverance, making them the continual subject of his public speeches and private conversation. This has certainly

tainly had the effect of substituting an almost-entire neglect of him in the House of Commons, in the place of the most perfect attention. A greater deference and respect was never paid to the most distinguished member.

I am, however, much more inclined to place this change of disposition to the fashionable levity of the times. Age and experience no longer attract respect. The minister is a very young man. He is supported by a long train of juvenile members, his companions. To these, and equally to those of the opposite party, whose minds are devoted to pleasure, such a conduct must be irksome. Others join in the same opinion, many from a good motive, an apprehension of its lessening the character of a man whom they highly value: but, in fact, it proceeds from the want of sufficient strength of mind to hear the continued pressure of even the most beneficial measures of Government.

Whatever

Whatever effects this quality may produce upon the present race of Englishmen, there is not a stronger and more incontestable proof of the character of a great man. Vast and comprehensive minds, who see the importance of objects, can never be at rest till they have investigated all their parts. These continual researches extend to their conversation in private, to all their actions in public life. Their whole thoughts are directed to these purposes, and they become insensible to every other employment that has not some great end in view.

In his temper he has not the smallest disguise, his great openness and simplicity often leading him to declare his sentiments with a freedom which all persons are not able to bear. In this manner he is a strong advocate for the coalition, and has avowed his sentiments very clearly upon that measure. His dislike of, I ought rather to say his disgust at, popular opinions has, perhaps, strengthened him

too

too much in attachments, which are not, strictly speaking, suitable to his own purity of mind.

In all important measures of Government he is clear, open, and determined. In the closet these qualities are essentially requisite; no man would conduct himself with greater propriety. In affairs of little moment, his natural desire to please would make him submit to the pleasure of the Crown; but in all the weighty measures of Government his opinions would be firm and explicit, his actions vigorous and decided.

I shall conclude the description of this great and valuable character by saying, that, although he has neither the advantages of great property or extensive connections, yet were he desired to take a lead in the administration of affairs, he would, doubtless, have the support of the Cavendishes, the Duke of Portland, Lord Fitzwilliam, and the other great Whig families,

lies, amply poffeffed of both. They refpect his virtues — they love his perfon.

I do not confider this to be a very improbable event, fhould this deferving perfon remain in England. In this time of
diftrefs, his long-acknowledged abilities
and integrity muft make him a capital object of attention. His mind is known to
be full of refources, and fuch a feafon
calls loudly for them. The nation has no
other character equally unexceptionable,
and in which the moft capacious and active powers of Government, inflexible integrity and private virtue, are fo happily
blended. There is another circumftance
which muft have its operation. This is
the neglect with which he has been treated
by fome of his party, who are perfonally
difliked in another quarter. The neareft
and moft intimate connection which a particular perfon enjoys, feems fully fenfible
of the neceffity of having a minifter who
has not only the firmnefs to expofe too-fa-
voured evils in their fulleft and moft odious

ous view, but the capacity to remove them.

My prefent employment is full of difficulty from the importance of the fubject, and full of delicacy from the peculiar fituation in which I ftand with this excellent perfon. I derive experience from a long and intimate connection, and I have employed it with the ftricteft regard to truth. My firft attachment to him arofe folely from principle; the continuance of it from affection and efteem. I felt it a duty, in taking leave of my country, to exprefs thefe my fentiments with fidelity and exactnefs. To defcribe a character is a voluntary act: and were I not fully fenfible that the failings (if I may make ufe of the expreflion) of this eminent perfon were merely the fudden flafhes of a great and generous mind, full of the moft tranfcendent virtues, I certainly fhould not have undertaken the employment: it would not have been that of a friend. It is now
the

the highest gratification which, in absence from him, I can receive.

I ought, however, to have premised, that my hopes and expectations wholly arise from the distress in which I foresee that one, to whom he owes all proper obedience, must be involved. In this situation, necessity is a law, to which the strongest must submit: and circumstances the most improbable have arisen from a complicated scene of confusion. Were not these the motives by which I have been influenced to offer my opinions, I should be deservedly stiled a writer of romance.

Any prince whatsoever might accomplish the purposes of ease to himself, his family, and his people, by vesting the administration of his affairs in the hands of such a man as I have here described — a man of integrity, of honour, of ability, supported by families of great property and extensive connections — in fine, possessed of those qualifications which, by

engaging

engaging the confidence of all honest men, would put an end to any distractions of the empire even in the moment of their arising, and timely guard against the calamities which, in such a case, would threaten the kingdom: and hence peace and happiness to the prince and people would certainly ensue. — Farewel.

From on board the Britannia, at sea, Nov. 1, 1784.

LETTER

LETTER IX.

ON THE

STATE OF THE COMMERCE

OF

GREAT BRITAIN

BEFORE THE WAR.

———— *Viresque acquirit eundo* ————
VIRG.

LETTER IX.

TO ——————

HAVING taken great pains to procure information of the state of our North-American and West-India commerce during a period of twenty years, and having paid a particular attention to the views and situation of the great continent which now constitutes the United States, I thought it proper to publish my opinions. I did it in a work entitled Considerations upon the present State of Great Britain and the United States of North America with respect to their future Commercial Connections. As this includes the chief part of what I have to say upon the North-American trade, it will be the means of contracting this letter, which is to treat of the present condition of our commerce, so far as it bears a relation to the circumstances of the government, and the state of our manners.

In a former letter I took notice of the great accession to our commerce during the war of 1756, by the possession of almost the whole of the colonial empire of France, and a valuable part of that of Spain, which, causing nearly the whole trade of those nations to center in our ports, filled them with purchasers from every part of Europe: and although many of our conquests were, in a manner, squandered away at the peace of 1762, we had yet a great increase of empire. Our American and West-India colonies grew to an immense size, notwithstanding the impolitic management which, as a part of the new system, was introduced into the colonial government.

Some of these regulations answering all the purposes of the French and Spanish Courts, who kept guarda costas in constant pay

pay to prevent the English colonists from trading with their subjects, appeared very strange in the system of a British government. These new arrangements were the ground work of the troubles with which the colonies were afterwards afflicted. From thence arose the burdensome and mischievous laws of the customs. The imposition of taxes and the long train of vexatious regulations followed. As I have already collected some materials, perhaps I may trouble you and the world with detached remarks upon this wretched system of commerce.

A view of the flourishing state of the empire, at this time, leads me to the observations which, in the letter that I have referred to, I made upon the subject of the funds. These, after all the fluctuations which attended the peace were over, settled at about ten per cent. under the par price of one hundred for the three per cents. The country having just emerged from an expensive war, required time to acquire a sufficient surplus of wealth to provide, as well for the improvements which were made in the kingdom, as for the purpose of raising the decreased value of the funds to its proper standard.

I consider this to be the cause why the funds did not rise to their standard: it confirms the opinion which I have already advanced, that, taking in all contingencies of Government, (particularly a bad system, which is long felt by posterity) if the national debt exceeds one hundred millions, it is attended with a burden injurious to the people, lessening the value of the public funds, and increasing the interest on the capitals employed in trade.

The prospects which appeared at the peace of 1762 were highly flattering. The increase of commerce and population in our colonies would have proved the means of producing this surplus, required for the advance of the funds, had not one of those contingencies happened to which I have

I have alluded. This contingency, which was the ſettlement of vaſt and unprofitable eſtates in the conquered iſlands in the Weſt Indies, chiefly Grenada, St. Vincent's, and Dominica, waſted ſuch immenſe ſums of money, that it produced, in the year 1772, the moſt diſtreſſing conſequences to the commercial intereſt.

A very large ſum of money was conſumed in theſe undertakings: the richeſt merchants in London ſunk under the weight of them. Banks had been erected for the purpoſes of circulation, to ſupply part of the money required. Many of thoſe were obliged to ſtop their payments, occaſioning heavy loſſes to the landed proprietors, who were obliged to make good the deficiencies. The conſternation into which all men of buſineſs were thrown, is a full proof of the magnitude of the diſtreſs which it occaſioned.

When a national debt has reached to that exceſs as to make its payment impracticable,

practicable, the only prudent step that remains is to confine it within bounds. Some politicians have discovered great advantage in a constant national debt. A temporary benefit was, perhaps, derived from it, when the family upon the throne was threatened by the house of Stuart; but these probable advantages are capitally overbalanced by very positive injuries. A national debt has many grievances. Amongst these, it burdens the manufacturer with taxes to maintain a vast body of idle people, who live upon the labour of the hive. They are the inactive drones of the State, and subsist upon the money which the public takes out of the pockets of the industrious to pay the interest for the debt it owes.

Had not the American war happened, the nation would have soon recovered the severe blow which it received in 1772. Her American colonies continued yearly to increase. Her ancient West-India plantations were greatly augmented in growth. The

The exports to North America had increased from 1,038,000 l. (including the African exports) the medium from 1739 to 1756, to 3,650,000 l. the medium of the three years preceding the war. Those to the West Indies, upon the same comparison, from 842,000 l. to 1,850,000 l. The North-American trade has been represented by some writers in such false colouring, as cannot fail to have an effect upon a people whose prejudices are too great to expect them to be easily undeceived.

Differing, upon commercial grounds, exceedingly from the opinions of Lord Sheffield, I cannot observe, without the utmost surprise, that he has ascribed the great convulsion amongst the merchants in 1772, to the losses which accrued from the American trade; and the rather, because several of the first families, who had connections with banks, had a very strong impression made upon their remembrance by by the delapidation of their estates, which were obliged to make good the loss.

I believe that it is yet generally remembered, that, in the case of evidence given to the House of Commons before the commencement of the war, one of the first North-American merchants in London declared at the bar, that he remembered but one bankruptcy of consequence in that trade; nor probably is it less known that the amount of all the debts due to the merchants, constituting the capital advanced to the Americans, was taken in the latter end of the year 1774, and was found to be six millions. The account was again taken, in the same manner, the latter end of 1775, and then proved to be only two millions, four millions having been discharged during the period in which these two accounts were taken. This fact is a very strong corroboration of the assertion made at that time by those of the American merchants who acted a fair and manly part, " that they had no other ap-
" prehension

" prehenfion for the debts due to them
" from America than from the meafures
" which had been adopted by Govern-
" ment."

This was the ftate of our colonial trade at that period. Our European commerce was alfo in a very flourifhing condition, though not in fuch a proportionate increafe. Our manufacturers had explored their way into almoft every part of the Continent of Europe. The manufacturers of Norwich, Manchefter, and Birmingham, kept the fairs in Italy, and Englifh riders to take orders for goods were to be met with in every capital town in Germany, and the North. Holland was the place of general rendezvous. In the Englifh inns of Amfterdam might be conftantly feen traders from Great Britain, who had taken the rout of almoft every nation in Chriftendom.

The view of an extenfive commerce affords the moft luxuriant reflections upon

its

its general utility to mankind. It combines nation with nation in the exchange of friendly offices, softens the most turbulent manners, and makes even the cruelty of war bend to its power. Kings, who, in former times, never made an excursion from their capital to a country seat without a legion of guards, now travel from one kingdom to another as private men.

The wealth which this extensive commerce brought into the kingdom preserved it even for a long time against the wretched government upon the new system. Continual inroads were, notwithstanding, made upon it by almost perpetual disputes with the North-American colonies, apparently designed to keep alive the flame of dissention, and to kindle a war upon the first favourable occasion. There is a quality in commerce, that of equalizing the different orders of a state by the means of the riches which it acquires, that is very favourable to liberty. This was consequently

quently offensive to some political characters, who, perhaps, wished to introduce a new system of government.

For a few years before the war with America commenced, the manufacturers had been so fully employed in the execution of orders from that country, as to leave some other branches of their trade without supply. When, therefore, the war began, and the American export ceased, they were, for a considerable time, engaged in the completion of their orders, both for the inland trade and for foreign parts. But when these branches of trade had received their regular supplies, and had taken their usual course, the manufacturers felt the want of employment, and would have been severe sufferers, had it not been for the trade of war, which then began to rise into importance.

The manufacturers who were chiefly affected were those of woollens, iron ware, nails, cutlery, glass, tobacco pipes, and all

all thofe articles, the confumption of which were chiefly confined to America. The manufactures of Norwich, Manchefter, Coventry, and thofe which depend upon fancy, had obtained fuch poffeffion of the inland and European trade, that they did not fuffer in any kind of proportion. I muft, however, except one branch of the Manchefter manufactory, the African trade.

The war was a vaft trade in itfelf, and employed many hands. The workmen in the different branches at Birmingham, Sheffield, and the iron countries, which fuffered by the war, were engaged in the cafting of cannon, the fabrication of guns, and other implements of deftruction. The contractor, the clothier, and the taylor, for the clothing of the different armies — the baker, the brewer, and all thofe who furnifhed provifions for their fupport — the rope maker, the fhip carpenter, the cooper, the fail maker, the fhip chandler, and the dependencies upon fhipping — the
owners

owners of ships freighted by Government, with a variety of other trades and professions, were all busily employed in the commerce of war.

The English were not aware that these circumstances would infallibly deprive them of all their ill-gotten profits : that such a compliance with them would not only be productive of burdensome taxes, but that, at the same time, the very means by which these taxes were to be paid would be equally reduced.

The candidates, however, for these employments rushed forward without fear of consequences. The member of Parliament who subscribed declarations against contracts, places, and pensions, could not muster up resolution to refuse a good offer for his ship, though it was to carry out soldiers for the purpose of prosecuting a war which he opposed. The merchant determined within himself, that if Government offered to give him a letter of marque

marque for his veffel, to make prize of the property of his fellow fubjects; others would accept it, fhould he refufe. The tradefman, who, in his nightly club, exclaimed againſt the American conteſt, ſpent his mornings in eager ſearch of orders for goods, which were to be employed in acts of hoſtility. Religion made no diſtinction. The Quaker, who prayed to God to preferve him from the ſin of paying his quota to the militia, who were to protect his country, manufactured gunpowder, and forged guns and ſwords, to deſtroy his fellow creatures.

Other manufacturers, who, for the want of ſuch a cuſtomer, had no orders to execute, continued to fill their warehouſes with manufactured goods, in the continual hope of an end being put to this unhappy war. Some of theſe goods were purchaſed by the merchants of Holland; but the far greater part was left in their hands.

The

The public having conceived an opinion that the difpofition of perfons apparently of great power and influence was very adverfe to grant independence to America, the news of the peace was rather unexpected; and not only the warehoufes of thofe who had manufactured on fpeculation, but of the manufacturers concerned for the war trade, (who had prepared great quantities, in expectation of another campaign) were full of goods. The effects which the peace produced upon our commerce fhall be the fubject of my next letter. — Farewel.

From on board the Britannia, at fea, the Anniverfary of the landing of King William, a glorious day for England, Nov. 4, 1784.

LETTER X.

ON THE

STATE OF THE COMMERCE

OF

GREAT BRITAIN

SINCE THE PEACE.

—— *Quid non mortalia pectora cogis,*
Auri sacra fames?
                              VIRG.

LETTER X.

TO ————————

————————

THE peace infused a new spirit into our commerce. Had the government, been then placed in hands which promised steadiness and permanency — had this season, so propitious to the revisal of our commerce, been properly improved — and had the American trade been regulated as nearly to its ancient system as the circumstances of the two nations would admit, Great Britain might, by degrees, have recovered from her losses: she might not have attained to that stupendous commerce, and to the great power which she formerly possessed, but she might yet have rendered herself a very respectable monarchy.

The very reverse happened in all respects. The people of the United States, who, in their colonial situation, had been the chief instrument of raising the mother country to her astonishing grandeur and riches, and who, from the instant that Great Britain had given her peace, shewed an inclination of reviving their old connections, were cast from us with a marked disdain. From being powerful fellow subjects, we now looked upon them as dangerous rivals, and viewed them with a jealous eye. Local and transitory resentments in any of the States were converted into fixed and inveterate prejudices of the whole union. The wild and unseemly vanity of some Americans, who visited the mother country, (there are a few who would have preserved the moderation of that people on their success) was substituted for the sense of a nation.

Solomon observes, that " jealousy is " the rage of a man :" — " A fool rageth " and is confident." This has been the
precise

precise situation of Great Britain. Envy and resentment have clouded her understanding, and made her blind to the benefits which she had formerly, and which she might still have enjoyed from a well-regulated connection with these rising States; but her vindictive pride has been her punishment. She has been ignorantly scattering with profusion the advantages in her possession, without the smallest attention to the mode of retribution, much less to profitable returns.

America had been exhausted by the war; and the natural consequences of this is, that she has not the capacity to pay for the quantities of goods which are necessary to her in the ruinous state to which she had been reduced.

On the other hand, the English warehouses were full of goods, and in great want of purchasers. The proprietors were not ignorant of the exhausted state of America. The old merchants, many of whom, by their conduct during the war, had difgufted their American correfpondents, and in whom the manufacturers and tradefmen had an habitual confidence, executed very few orders. The few American merchants were moftly unknown, and the orders which they gave, greatly exceeding their known or even reputed property, made thofe who were to fupply the goods eftimate the rifque of trufting them at a high rate.

This rifque was ftill farther increafed by the prohibitory proclamations. Thefe put a ftop to various modes of remittances, which were formerly directly and circuitoufly fent to the Britifh merchant in payment for the manufactures which the Americans purchafed of him.

The refufal, in effect, by thefe proclamations, of capital fums in payment for the goods with which the Britifh Government fuffered her merchants to fupply the Americans,

Americans, arose from speculative politicians.

These gentlemen amused themselves with building castles in the air, which were to hold thousands of future exporters of lumber and provisions from the inhospitable wilds of Canada and Nova Scotia, and a long additional train of ship builders and fishermen in Great Britain. The climate of those countries would soon convert the castles of such politicians into ice, and congeal the blood of their fancied inhabitants; or, if it were possible, that, by squandering away immense sums of money, we could cut down the forests, and fill the country with people, they would cease to be subjects.

In either case, it is a destructive speculation. For, with respect to our future fisheries, if we have not sufficient industry to maintain a superiority over those of America, which are at three thousand miles distance, and from thence formerly supplied

supplied our markets with oil, we shall never exceed our present bounds. As to our ship carpenters, their price is now so great as to render the holding a property in ships of no profit.

It is ridiculous to mention the carrying trade, for which such a clamour had been raised. Our folly has left us no other part than that which we can restrain by law. This will be a poor restraint, a mere spider's web, if the merchant does not find it his interest to obey it.

The merchants in America who had specie, sent it in payment for the goods which they ordered. They were, therefore, readily supplied. There were, however, few in this situation: the orders in general were, therefore, executed upon long credit. The warehouses being crowded with goods, was the single temptation to fulfil the orders received in this manner. The precaution which they took to lessen the risque, was to charge the goods
which

which they supplied at a higher price than usual.

All trade, which has not an equivalent capital to support it, is carried on in the spirit of adventurous gambling, the effects of which are not felt till the day of payment approaches. The apprehensions of the merchants first sound the alarm; those of the manufacturers and tradesmen follow, and are quickly spread abroad. These symptoms have already appeared in London. The consequences which must soon appear will probably prove fatal to great numbers. There has not been an administration since the peace (we have had them in rapid succession) to whom these consequences have not been distinctly pointed out, and who have not been repeatedly told that a judicious settlement of the American commerce would, in a great measure, prevent them.

The Americans, as I have already observed, were not able to make immediate payment

payment for the great quantity of goods which they imported. The confequence has been, that though fome of the early importations were fold well, the fubfequent ones have met with very few purchafers, except at fuch long credit as will probably prove, in the end, deftructive both to buyer and feller. A great part had been fold at auction, and fent into the interior parts of the country. The loffes which will attend thefe importations muft fall ultimately upon the manufacturer in Great Britain who fupplied the goods.

It is very probable that the dreadful profpect which opens itfelf to Great Britain will be foon matured. The two great wounds, which the commercial part of it may expect, will be received from the Eaft-India Company, and the American merchants. Of the latter, enough has been faid: the former cannot be mentioned without horror.

The real proprietors have no authority left: their servants are become their masters. The common forms of trade are too frigid and contracted for the far greater part of these gentlemen. They have a much more facile method of making their fortunes. This is the trade of plunder, which they first squeeze out of the miserable inhabitants, and then squander their wealth at home; a part in necessary bribes for protection, and the remainder in corrupting the manners of the people by the most wanton profusion.

The present Administration, who are their avowed protectors, have loaded the people with taxes for the support of the East-India Company, or, more properly speaking, for the support of their clients, the servants of that Company. The money which that Company owed to Government for the payment of duties, is commuted by a window tax, to be paid by the people at large. This commutation is for the duties which the Company formerly

merly paid upon their tea. Surely that poisonous weed has been already sufficiently destructive. Tea has ruined both the constitution and the manners of half the kingdom; tea was one great cause of the loss of America; and tea will now, in all probability, bring home to the door of Great Britain the mischief which she has caused it to produce in America.

The condition of the affairs of the Company both in England and the East — the large debts due to Government and private people — the immense value of the bills which are under their acceptance, and unpaid — and the investments for remittances, swallowed up in the enormous wealth of their servants, to whom the Company are now merely factors, are so many clear proofs of absolute and ruinous bankruptcy. The people, who have been plundered by the present ministers to pay their duties and their dividends, are still to be plundered to pay off their debts, in order to re-establish re-eſtabliſh this monopoly for farther oppreſſion and diſtreſs.

It has been the cauſe of much ſpeculation, whether the Europeans have ever carried on a productive trade with the Eaſt Indies. That extenſive country, poſſeſſing every advantage that can be derived from climate, abounds with people who are amply ſupplied not only with the neceſſaries, but even the luxuries of life. The mildneſs of the climate, and the forms both of their religion and government, aſſiſted by a natural ingenuity of mind, diſpoſe them to domeſtic employments: hence they have ſome of the moſt beautiful fabrics in the world; and thus are the products of the Eaſt Indies ſufficient not only for the conſumption of the inhabitants, but for the purpoſes of export. The trade, therefore, with that country, from the earlieſt accounts in hiſtory, has been carried on by the trafficking the ſilver of Europe for the manufactures and luxuries of the Eaſt.

This

This was the manner in which the trade to the East Indies was formerly carried on by the ancients. The merchandize was chiefly transported by the way of the Caspian and Euxine seas, which were then surrounded by a fertile and populous country, full of great and powerful cities. This communication extended to almost the whole of the East-India trade. The commerce of Egypt was at that time confined to the Red sea, and the different cities on the Malabar coast, as far south as the island of Ceylon, beyond which the ancients never navigated. The Romans, when they became masters of Egypt, greatly extended the trade through this channel.

The wars between the Romans and Parthians first obstructed the channel of communication by the Caspian and Euxine seas; and the irruptions of the Tartars having entirely depopulated its beautiful coast, the trade centered wholly in Egypt.
Alexandria

Alexandria was the principal market for the merchandize of the East.

The commerce continued to be confined to this city after the destruction of the eastern empire. The Venetians became the principal purchasers of their valuable commodities, which they afterwards distributed through Europe, deriving enormous profits from this traffic. Venice, by these means, became one of the most powerful states in Europe.

The last change was produced by the discovery of the Cape of Good Hope. How long the trade will continue in its present state, or whether it will fall back into its ancient channel through Egypt, (a much more natural communication) is a matter of doubt. It will, however, be carried on, in some shape, by individuals, so long as there remains money in Europe to purchase the luxuries of India.

The question for the national confideration is, whether the trade is beneficial or unproductive? It muſt certainly have been unproductive to the ancients, fince they derived but a comparatively fcanty fupply of filver from the mines in their poffeffion. The Indian commodities were indeed fold at an immenfe profit; but this was only a partial advantage to the merchant who carried on the trade. The nation was no otherwife benefited than by the increafe of its navigation, which we may fuppofe did not bear a proportion to the inconveniences which it fuffered by being drained of its fpecie. We are affured of this circumftance, that as the luxuries of Rome increafed, almoſt the whole of which were brought from Afia and the Eaft, the fcarcity of filver was marked by the proportionate bafenefs of the coin.

The moſt natural channel between Europe and the Indies appears to be through Egypt, which is the proper entrepot for the

the commodities of the East. The manners of the Turks are somewhat softened, and perhaps some great revolution in Asia may take place. This is an age of extraordinary events. In Europe, there are very strong appearances of a revolution in politics. The little States, which have hitherto subsisted upon the jealousy of their great neighbours, will soon become a sacrifice to these potent rivals.

The present European companies will not be able long to maintain their ground; it is, therefore, more than probable that an end, at least for some time, will be put to the tedious and expensive voyages round the Cape of Good Hope. The uniform experience which we have had of the failure of success in every East-India Company in Europe, seems to point out the probability of this event.

I shall not, in this place, take the conduct of the servants of the Companies into consideration, but merely examine the principles upon which this commerce is carried on. The voyages round the Cape of Good Hope (as I have already obferved) are tedious and expenfive. The paffage, on the contrary, through Egypt, is fhort and expeditious. The latter circumftance has alfo another, and a very capital advantage. This arifes from the fituation of Egypt, which forms a very happy entrepot for the commodities of both Europe and the Eaft.

An entrepot, in a medium fituation, is an object of great importance to the merchants of both countries. They perform their voyages to the place of rendezvous with greater eafe; their bufinefs is much fooner difpatched; and they have the fatisfaction of returning with greater expedition. A voyage to the Eaft Indies is now a work of years; the inconvenience of which is continually increafing, according to its extent, in multiplied proportions.

Another

Another disadvantage attending this trade is, the carrying it on by means of bullion only. I am sensible that the export of silver is not productive of the same inconveniences to the moderns as were felt by the ancients; the discovery of America having afforded such an ample supply of that commodity as to occasion a very considerable increase in its value.

The export of silver to the East Indies has been even represented to be of advantage, by preventing a greater accumulation in Europe, which would otherwise, by the continual import from America, abound too much with that commodity for the purposes of commerce. A great reduction of the value of money under its present standard, would be the means of lessening the value of merchandize. The transportation is attended with a heavy expence. This would increase, and might, by degrees, swallow up the profit.

Gold and silver are chosen as the medium of commerce, because they are scarcer than any other metal, and therefore more portable. If they could be procured in equal quantities, some other distinction must be invented.

But should the export of bullion to the East Indies prove, in this view, an advantage to Europe in general, yet the trade, partially considered with respect to particular nations, will be productive of either good or ill effects, according to their different circumstances. Spain and Portugal appear to be very striking instances in proof of this assertion. They are the proprietors of all the gold and silver mines, yet a very small proportion belongs to them. The Spaniards do not retain a twentieth part of the bullion which they import.

They have not a sufficient quantity of goods for the supply of their colonies. They are obliged to suffer the different nations

nations in Europe to send them manufactures, which they transport to the Indies, where they are exchanged for specie. This precious commodity, which is first conveyed to Spain, is the profitable return made to the proprietors in re-payment for these goods. The discovery of the riches of the Indies has proved of essential injury to the mother country. Mexico and Peru are, in fact, no longer her property. They are become the general property of those nations which carry on the trade, by providing the goods necessary for the consumption of the inhabitants.

The advantage or injury from the East-India trade to a particular state, therefore, wholly depends upon circumstances. Venice derived both power and riches from this trade.

The high price of the funds in England before the war of 1756, and the very moderate interest she then paid, afforded no appearances of injury from the export of silver

silver by the East-India Company. That Company then acted in their proper capacity, as a body of merchants. On the contrary, the present low price of our funds, the scarcity of money, and the high interest we pay for it, are evident marks of the necessity of restraining this trade. All circumstances, therefore, now combine to support the opinion, that the East-India trade is unprofitable and destructive.

A nation, in the situation of Great Britain, loaded with an immense debt, its credit great and extensive, the medium of its commerce, notwithstanding a large quantity of specie, requiring an enormous paper circulation, and whose Bank notes supply the place of coin, has every thing to fear from the consequences of the violent convulsions with which it is threatened. They may be properly compared to a dreadful conflagration, which the want of water suffers to rage with ungovernable

vernable fury, without any poffibility of fixing the bounds of its extent.

One great confequence cannot fail to be produced — that of emigration. When I have treated of the manners of the people, which have been the primary caufe of all their calamities, I fhall take this subject into confideration. — Farewel.

From on board the Britannia, at fea,
Nov. 6, 1784.

LETTER XI.

UPON THE

FORMER AND PRESENT STATE

OF THE

MANNERS OF THE PEOPLE

OF

GREAT BRITAIN.

Privatis illis cenſus erat brevis,
Commune magnum.
HOR.

CICERO, in his letters to Atticus, written a few years before the government of the Roman republic was usurped by Cæsar, describes very much the manners of our times, in the account which he gives to his friend of the transactions at Rome. There are some expressions in them which more particularly apply to my present subject—" *Sed dolor est ma-* " *jor, cum videas civitatis voluntatem so-* " *lutam, virtutem alligatam***." The good citizen of our days will deplore, with equal grief and indignation, the licentious-

---

* But how much more woeful is it, when we consider that the spirit of our countrymen is unbraced, and their virtue choaked?
Guthrie's Translation.

ness

ness which so generally prevails amongst his countrymen, and the indifference, or, rather, contempt, in which virtue is considered amongst them. Rome was then, what Great Britain is now, in a very willing disposition to receive a master.

There are many points in which the two nations have an agreement. They were both famous, in the better days of their government, for a stubborn virtue bordering upon ferociousness, and a love of liberty reaching to enthusiasm. The example of this great people, when under the influence of luxury and licentiousness of manners, points out to us the ease with which a transition is made from these vices to the most abject servility. Rome was distinguished for this base quality, after it had lost its liberty. Great Britain, similar in disposition, when its people were freemen, will be similar in disposition should they become slaves.

The

The judicial part of our Conſtitution is certainly leſs corrupt. Whenever the private property of the ſubject has been in queſtion, the conduct of the judges, in our times, has been without blemiſh.

The principal cauſes which produced the preſent diſſolute manners throughout the nation, have ariſen within theſe few years. Formerly they were confined to the capital; but ſince the great roads have been repaired, new ones made, and the communication with the moſt diſtant parts of the kingdom rendered eaſy, theſe manners have been generally introduced. In ſome parts, where the natural bluntneſs of manners have received only a finer edge and poliſh, the effects have been good. The taverns have been leſs, the ſociety of women (without whom there can be no true reliſh of life) more frequented. Amongſt theſe their manners have been improved, and rendered more ſociable. In other parts, the moſt brutal vices of the capital have rendered the inhabitants, if possible, still more brutal; and, in some places, an excess of a higher kind of debauchery, and the more expensive refinements of luxurious living, have been mixed with the lowest vices.

The manners of those whose rough dispositions admitted a polish by a more social intercourse with the world, were improved, generally speaking, without injury to their estates. If some amongst them have fallen, others have arisen to supply their places. But men, who have merely imbibed the brutal vices of the capital, have been not only rendered still more disgusting by the increase of their natural vices, but also by the increase of their low cunning and fraudulent desire of gain. Whilst it may be said of those amongst whom the debaucheries, both of the first and of the lowest rank, have been received, that expensive living, dress, and love of pleasure of every kind, have destroyed their natural industry, made them neglect their business, and ultimately operated

rated as the means of producing a general ruin.

The fashions of the town, which formerly travelled only once or twice a year with the judges on the circuit, or with the principal persons of the country, when they returned from London, are brought down almost daily by the stage coaches, which now travel, night and day, from the capital even to the Highlands of Scotland, the mountains of Wales, and the extremity of Cornwall. Fashions not being very congenial to the grave body of the law, the men of the country were very flow in their approaches. Women, to whom the improvement of their persons is more natural, and indeed laudable, when kept within proper bounds, made a greater progress in imitating them. The Spectator (the " *magister morum*" of the age in which he wrote) has described some circumstances which relate to this subject with great humour.

In the city of London a sobriety of manners then prevailed. The police was more strictly kept up, the hours regular, and the manners of the citizens, both in their dress and in their tables, were consistent with their professions. A line of distinction still remained between the city and the west end of the town. Few of the merchants or principal people in trade resided there.

The manners of people of rank and distinction were more particularly their own. They were seldom to be seen without some degree of splendour; and they preserved a form in their appearance which inspired their inferiors with respect. An attention both to dress and address was necessary to every person who paid even a morning visit to men of distinction.

These appearances, which commanded personal respect and attention, were confined to men of rank, whilst those which sprung from riches were generally distributed

buted through the kingdom. There was much real wealth in the country. Most families possessed a considerable quantity of plate and jewels, silks, linen, and other valuable moveables. These descended from father to son, and from mother to daughter. The plate was massy, the linen fine and durable, the silks rich and weighty. Purchases were then made for posterity. These appeared only on public occasions, or in families upon a marriage, christening, or any such extraordinary festivals. The ornaments were costly; and were not so much the property of the temporary possessor as the property of his family.

Our manners, considered as a people, had no material change before the influx of wealth after the peace of 1763. The alterations made in them by the increase of our commerce proceeding from the acquisitions of the war, were generally so many improvements. The corruption arose from the plunder of our territorial empire in the East. We have only to recur to the last

last thirty years to prove this difference. In 1756 we had a full experience of the manly conduct of the English nation, when it beheld its honour wounded by the capture of the paltry island of Minorca. Some intervals of the period from the commencement of the year 1762, to the close of the year 1766, were marked by strong appearances of popular indignation against proceedings which were considered as tyrannical; and hence may we infer, without meaning to enter upon a disquisition concerning either the justice or the impropriety of their emotions, that the multitude was not destitute of either a quick sense of supposed injury, or an impatient spirit of opposition. During the American war, the people, apparently sunk almost into indifference, saw coolly the approaching separation of one part of the empire from the other, as if, with thoughtless generosity, they could have forgiven the ignorance and impolicy of those statesmen whose baneful measures contributed to the division.

The riches which flowed into the kingdom from the acquisitions made in the war of 1756, were laudably appropriated to public improvements. The lands of the kingdom were fertilized — barren heaths enclosed — the country covered with new and beautiful edifices — almost new cities were ingrafted upon the capital and other principal towns — canals were digged which united sea to sea, promoting an inland trade, and producing to those parts of the kingdom (which were distressed for them) plenty of coals, lime, and other necessaries for use and improvement. Happy would it be for a people, could the distribution of its riches be confined within proper bounds! But such were the effects of the plunder of the East in corrupting our manners, that we very soon made a rapid stride from the laudable improvements to the most corrupt and licentious conduct. My next letter will be upon that subject. — Farewel.

From on board the Britannia, at sea,
Nov. 10, 1784.

LETTER XII.

THE CONTINUATION OF THE SAME SUBJECT;

CHIEFLY UPON THE

CHANGE

WHICH THE

EAST-INDIA WEALTH

PRODUCED IN OUR MANNERS.

―――――

―――― *Quid nos dura refugimus*
Ætas? Quid intactum nefasti
Liquimus? Unde manum juventus
Metu deorum continuit?
      Hor.

THE wealth of the Indies, too generally procured by rapine, and spent with profusion, gave the first great shock to our manners. When the East-India Company ceased to act in the spirit of a commercial body, and the battle of Plaffey had laid the foundation of their sovereignty in the East, the greater part of their servants acted no longer in the station of traders. Formerly, confining themselves merely to that profession, they retired to England with the fruits of their labours. This was either early or late in life, according to their ideas of sufficiency. With some they were very moderate. In that time of order, (the gradation of rank to the high post of Governor itself being perfectly regular)

gular) the fortunes brought home by even thofe of the firſt power and dignity were very rarely to be called exceſſive.

But when the fervants were taught the facile method of dethroning the fovereigns of the country, all order was fubverted.

It has been ſtrongly infinuated, that when the power of appointing to the principal departments of the Government of India paſſed into another channel, the different Refidencies in the Eaſt for the collection of the revenue, and all other places of emolument, were, in a manner, fet up for fale. Many (how truly, let the reader judge) concluded that the former regularity of the fervice, affording a certainty to the fervant to rife to the higheſt rank, (a cuſtom, till that time, religiouſly preferved) was laid afide, and inferred as (being in their idea) a natural confequence, that the principal fervants made their bargains in one powerful quarter, and their inferior fervants, in another, poſſeſſed of

almoſt

almost equal efficacy; by which means (as they concluded) there was scarce a district in India that was not plundered without mercy. Granting, for the sake of argument, the validity of this position, we might draw an imaginary picture, and represent simitars, rings, bracelets, stomachers, and other equally-valuable jewels, torn out of the mines in the East Indies, and brought in haste to ornament the persons of some of the most fashionable and exalted members of the community in England. True it is, that, on some occasions, the most rapid fortunes were made in an instant; and that when an inferior servant appeared, who had interest at home, or could in any shape, by his connections, render service to some particular individuals, his fortune was certainly made. Various methods were adopted for these purposes: sometimes by robberies committed upon the princes and people in India; sometimes by robberies committed upon the East-India Company, and the people of England, in the shape of iniquitous

tous contracts. For the firſt there was no ceremony uſed: for the laſt, forms were always preſerved.

It has been ſurmiſed, that, in ſome flagrant caſes relative to contracts for tranſporting produce, a ſervant, either in the civil or the military line, not according to the nature of the ſervice, but according to the purpoſes to be ſerved, offers a ſhip; that another offers guns; another ſtores; another is appointed commander; others are ſupercargoes. In many of theſe contracts this parade is ſaid to have been actually made, merely to provide for a number of favourites, there being no market exiſting that could take off the produce thus ſent to it. There it periſhes, and the charges are placed to the Company's account.

In ſuch a ſituation it muſt follow, that the poor ſervant who does his duty, but has no intereſt, and whoſe conſcience will not ſuffer him to get money in ſo profligate

a man-a manner, is left to starve upon his place, without being able to pay even the expence of his living. If this be true, with what justice can we arraign the conduct of the Roman governors, who fleeced, with the most cruel tyranny, the provinces of the empire? Have we, or have we not, heard of Englishmen reviving the same tyranny over the peaceable and unhappy Indians?

If it be indisputable that the vices of Asia have reached England, and that a great and immediate change has taken place in our manners, it may be doubted whether the East Indians were not men of low extraction, brought up either in the camp to insolence and plunder, or in office, to the accumulation of money by indirect practices. Such men, at a time when a very strong desire of enjoyment increased with the national wealth, must have proved dangerous intruders. In the habit of amassing money at pleasure, and of spending it with profusion, they must have shewn themselves totally ignorant of

its

its value; and hence would it follow, that magnificent palaces muſt ariſe, in which taſte and ſituation were not ſo much conſulted as expence. Upon this gronnd, it were natural to obſerve, that the views of the Eaſt Indians were to diſplay their riches with oſtentation; and that for this purpoſe they made one general attack upon the nobility and gentry, and all the opulent part of the kingdom.

To purſue the image, one might remark, that whilſt they thus rivalled them in their buildings, their tables, and their dreſs, they contended with them in another favourite purſuit, the defire of a feat in Parliament; that the boroughs in general were filled either with the neighbouring country gentlemen, or candidates recommended by men of rank or eſtate, who had either the property of, or great influence in, them; that theſe conteſts were generally warmly diſputed; that it often happened, that, though the Engliſhman involved his eſtate, his Eaſt-India antagoniſt gonift spent till he could spend no longer; and, though reduced to bankruptcy, by interest procured a fresh appointment, in order to procure fresh plunder.

How would an impartial writer treat this odious subject? Would he not say, that the ancient nobility and the men of rank felt themselves much hurt at this rivalship of new men, whose only good quality consisted in possessing vast sums of money? And thus probably would he continue his remarks:—" All those distinc-
" tions which separated them from their
" inferiors, were now in danger of being
" lost; they, therefore, made a stand,
" and encountered them with their own
" expensive weapons: but at length they
" found the contest too powerful for their
" estates to support, and many sunk under
" the burden.

" The example soon spread itself through
" all ranks of people, and produced very
" disagreeable effects. Many of the gen-
" try

" try had been induced by the goodness of
" the roads to spend their winters in town.
" This subjected them to an increased ex-
" pence, and rendered them little able to
" bear any addition; yet such was the in-
" fluence of this infectious disease, that
" they rushed headlong into every excess.
" Nor was the disorder confined to the
" town only. They carried with them
" into the country the same taste for ex-
" pence, exciting a dangerous emulation
" in those who had hitherto the wisdom
" to live upon their estates.

" As all inhabitants of warm climates
" are addicted to indolence and extrava-
" gance, it was not surprising that the
" West Indies (whose plantations had been
" greatly increased since the peace of 1763,
" and who were now possessed of large
" incomes) should eagerly embrace a man-
" ner of life so much adapted to their na-
" tural dispositions. It was not, how-
" ever, so congenial to the grave body of
" merchants and traders of London, who
" yet

" yet plunged into all the vices of the
" age as far as their abilities could be
" ſtretched; many far beyond them. The
" principal towns were not long in follow-
" ing theſe dangerous precedents; and
" thus did the whole kingdom ruſh into
" diſſipation, luxury, and licentiouſneſs.

" The minds of the people being thus
" weakened, it was not a difficult matter
" to perſuade them that their duty did not
" extend beyond their own concerns; that
" an attention to the national affairs was
" an interference which did not become
" them; and that the care of the State
" ought to be left to thoſe whom the
" Court, in their wiſdom, ſhould think
" proper to appoint."

Such, were the occaſion to ariſe, would prove the remarks of an impartial, but indignant, inveſtigator; and, indeed, for their ſupport, he might, independently of their general conduct, make an unanſwerable appeal to a late advertiſement of ſome of the principal merchants in London upon the difmiffion of the Portland Adminiftration. An advertifement of men, who, in other refpects, have acted with a proper fenfe of the dignity of their fituation.— " The merchants, or traders, who think " the appointment or difmiffion of His " Majefty's minifters not a fubject for their " interference, are acquainted that a paper " to that effect is now ready for their fig- " natures."

I fhall be now juftified in adding another quotation from Cicero, written a few years after the period in which the firft was made, fince it is very applicable to this fubject. He fays to Atticus, * " *Multum* " *mecum municipales homines loquuntur, mul-* " *tum rufticani; nihil prorfum aliud curant,* " *nifi agros, nifi villulas, nifi nummulos fuos.*"

---

* I have had a good deal of talk with our townf-men, and a great deal with our country gentlemen in thefe quarters, and, take my word for it, they have no concern but about their lands, their farms, and their money.

Guthrie's Tranflation.

—If

—If I were to give an account of the state of our country, I should equally say, I have conversed with many of our citizens, and many of our country gentlemen and farmers: they pay no regard to any thing but their estates, their farms, and their money.

The improvements which were carried into execution in London, and the principal towns, had been the occasion of great additions in buildings. Originally, in London, it was partly to provide for those new inhabitants who came from the country to spend the winter in town, and partly to afford some elbow room to those who were confined to close habitations. Convenience was then chiefly studied; but, at this time, it gave place to magnificence, and houses were built and finished in the most expensive taste.

Such was the effect which the alteration of our manners had upon all ranks, that these splendid mansions were not only occupied

cupied by families from the country, but by merchants and opulent tradesmen. The former, from making use of lodgings in their occasional visits to town, at length settled in houses. Mere convenience would not, however, now satisfy them. The latter, who had been formerly contented with their houses in the city, in which their families resided, and where their business was carried on, now rented a large costly fabric at the west end of the town. The house in the city was turned into a compting house, and that commerce which, by the industry and knowledge of the trader, had formerly been productive of much national wealth, was now looked upon with contempt by the fine gentleman, and left to be managed by inexperienced clerks. — My next letters will be upon the ill effects which this change of manners has produced in the limited monarchy of England. — Farewel.

From on board the Britannia, at sea,
    Nov. 12, 1784.

LETTER

LETTER XIII.

THE SAME SUBJECT CONTINUED;

PARTICULARLY WITH RESPECT TO THE

INFLUENCE

WHICH THE

NEWSPAPERS

HAVE HAD IN

CORRUPTING OUR MANNERS.

Fecundæ culpæ fecula nuptias
Primum inquenavere, et genus, et domos;
Hoc fonte derivata clades
In patriam populumque fluxit.
      Hor.

LETTER XIII.

TO ――――

A PROPER equality is necessary to the welfare of a republic. The distinction of nobility is necessary to the welfare of a monarchy. England is a limited monarchy; yet it partakes so much more of the latter than of the former government, that it is contrary to her true interests to suffer the dignity of her nobility to be degraded. A very manifest difference in the respect paid to the peerage has been shewn in our times. Variety of causes are assigned for this change. Many impute it to the increased power and riches of the commercial part of the kingdom, which, they say, brings the state of our monarchy nearer to that of a republic. But this circumstance, had our manners been less corrupt,

corrupt, could have made no inroad upon the honours of nobility. The State, in general, would have been benefited, and the merchant or trader, as he grew rich, would have been converted into a country gentleman, to fupply the places of thofe who were obliged to fell their eftates to fatisfy their creditors.

The caufes of their prefent declenfion appear to me to be thefe:—Firft, an ill-timed pique at the rivalfhip of fuch obfcure men as the Eaft Indians; which, having involved them in immenfe expences, has funk their eftates, and rendered them neceffitous and dependent; and next, fuch frequent creations of nobles, during a feries of preceding years, as nearly doubled the Lords of both kingdoms, and, in confequence, leffened their influence and dignity in the opinion of the world.

When the nobility found themfelves worfted in the conteft of expence, they had no longer the hope of preferving the particular

particular diftinctions in appearance which they formerly enjoyed; they, therefore, threw off the bandages of ftate, and mixed with freedom in the world: they walked the ftreets, generally wore a plain drefs, and laid afide, both in their own appearance and in their carriages, that fplendour by which they had been formerly diftinguifhed. Their tables were frequented with greater freedom, and it was fufficient to have the manners of a gentleman to be admitted to them.

It is pleafant to have the privilege of entering the houfe of a man of the firft rank without parade, with the fame freedom of drefs as we fhould enter into that of an equal: even the etiquette of drefs at dinner is now fo much abated, that it can hardly be faid to be kept up even in a few of the winter months. Many, who preferve it, act merely from a preferable defire of fhewing, to a fear of being thought to want, refpect. In the moft auguft affembly which we have, the Houfe of Lords,

Lords, many of them appear in an undrefs. That Gothic ornament, the fword, is nearly difcarded: it is retained chiefly at Court.

The manners of the nobility have had a good effect with refpect to drefs, and convenience continues ftill to fupport it; but the nation was too far plunged into a tafte for expence in general to retain this fimplicity in any mode of living, unlefs their convenience was particularly confulted. The coftlinefs of our houfes, tables, carriages, and harnefs, are greater in thefe times than ever.

As the inundation of the Eaft-India profufion, at a time when we had ourfelves acquired fome habits of expence, firft made an alteration in our manners, I confider the newfpapers as the means by which this change was encouraged and fupported.

About twenty-five years ago there were only three daily newfpapers in London. They

They were generally filled with foreign news and transactions of the country. The miscellaneous part contained either strictures on Government, or letters of amusement. Strictures upon Government, when kept within the bounds of decency, are useful to a free people. The administrations of those times were vigilant in their endeavours to prevent the licentiousness of the press. Whenever any paper exceeded the limits of propriety, the author and publisher were immediately prosecuted, and seldom escaped punishment.

The foreign news giving them an idea of the state of public affairs on the Continent, Englishmen had then some knowledge of the politics of Europe. Country news made them acquainted with the transactions at home.

There are at this time nine daily papers. They certainly ought not to be stiled newspapers, for they give us little or no news: they subsist upon political paragraphs, which,

which, by perplexing the mind, prevent decifion upon public principles, rendering each party equally difgufting — upon an abufe of private character, deftroying that fenfe of reputation which preferves appearances in the world, and mingling both the good and the bad in one mafs — and upon the propagation of vices through the kingdom, holding forth thofe for imitation which would otherwife have been concealed within the circle of their commiffion.

It has been the general experience of all ages, that a corruption of manners in the women is the prelude to the fall of a nation. We have had mournful proofs of the increafe of this diforder in our age; nor is there any caufe to which it can be more juftly attributed than to the indifcriminate manner in which the newfpapers difcufs female characters. Women of reputation are abufed and vilified. The manner in which fufpected characters are exhibited, generally produces an effect upon their

their conduct which renders them no longer doubtful. Proftitutes of diftinction are held forth as objects of admiration. The defcription which the newfpapers give of thefe characters excites in every proftitute, who is not wholly abandoned, a thorough contempt of the public opinion, and a wanton defire of throwing off all appearances, fetting modefty completely at defiance. Proftitutes are evils which are by fome deemed neceffary in a great kingdom. If this fhould even be the cafe, they cannot be fuffered with too much filence and precaution.

Befides, the very communication of thofe vices in newfpapers has a tendency to produce corruption of manners even in the moft virtuous part of the fex. Female frailties fometimes require the full force of education and principle to refift and correct them; yet narrations are often given in the newfpapers in the moft indecent terms. The ear of a modeft woman, at firft a ftranger to them, is ftruck by the

constant

constant repetition. They raise curiosity, and occasion inquiry, till, by degrees, she grows familiarised to them. She then searches for those suspected characters of her own sex who are most likely to conduce to her gratification. I will draw a veil over many unhappy women who have, in this manner, fallen a prey. Happy are those who do not suffer their curiosity to lead them on to criminal thoughts. From thence the transition is soon made to criminal actions.

Another evil has arisen from the general abuse of character. Juries seem to have laid down a rule, that the newspapers are now so infamous, that no credit can be given to them, and, therefore, that a person whose character is defamed in them, can receive no injury. This dangerous doctrine affords an unbounded licence to the editors of newspapers, and gives them an unlimited sanction of general abuse: they are, therefore, under no restraint, for Government will not interfere. The Court

Court confiders that an univerfal licentioufnefs in the prefs will lead to a defire of univerfal reftraint; but the people ought to confider that this evil will be equally intolerable.

The converting the newfpapers from being vehicles of foreign and domeftic intelligence into vehicles of fcandal and abufe, has deftroyed that knowledge which the Englifh formerly poffeffed of the ftate of the Continent and of its politics. The people know almoft as much of the Emperor of Japan as they do of the Emperor of Germany. The want of this political knowledge producing an indifference to the ftate of our own affairs, and an increafe of thofe vices which weaken the body and debafe the mind, has given a new turn to fociety. Our converfations are no longer directed to manly fubjects. Women, gaming, drefs, fafhions, and eating and drinking, as they employ our time without doors, fill up the meafure of our converfation within.

There

There are no ranks of people in Great Britain who do not, in some measure, participate of these vices. If we look to the nobility and men of distinction, there are very few indeed who merit our respect. I am sorry to say that the words of Cicero are too applicable to the far greater part—
" *Quibus optimatibus dii boni? Qui nunc quo*
" *modo occurrunt quo modo autem se vendi-*
" *tant Cæsari*.*"

But what can be expected from men whose highest joy is in the richness of their dress, the gilding of their carriages, or the gaudy trappings of their horses; or, which forms to many a yet more exquisite pleasure, in some new dish, or highly-seasoned sauce, whose relish they contemplate with the most curious and grateful attention?

To support the comparison which I have formed between the manners of Britain

---

* Of what quality, immortal gods! See how they flock, see how they sell off themselves to Cæsar.
Guthrie's Translation.

and

and Rome, I ought to quote the words of Ammianus Marcellinus, who has left us some remarkable accounts of those of his time; but, referring you to the passage itself, I have a pleasure in giving you those of an elegant, sensible, and accurate describer of the manners of our days, which equally respects this subject. The amiable writer, in her Evelina, has the following words: " After this, the conversation
" turned wholly upon eating, a subject
" which was discussed with the utmost
" delight; and had I not known that they
" were men of rank and fashion, I should
" have imagined that they had all been
" professed cooks; for they displayed so
" much knowledge of sauces and made
" dishes, and of the various methods of
" dressing the same things, that I am
" persuaded they must have given much
" time and much study to make them-
" selves such adepts in the art."

The losses which we sustained during the war were the lessons of adversity, which

which it was our duty to make profitable to us; but our hearts have been callous, and we have no sense of proper feeling. They have produced no other effects in us than absurd ideas of impotent and unmanly resentment. To debasement of manners we have added its natural consequence, servility of mind. Instead of entering with manly resolution into the state of our affairs, and using our best endeavours to retrieve them, we wilfully shut our eyes to the truth. We continue bewildered in that labyrinth of errors which has already involved us in great difficulties; and if we do not speedily find some clue to get out, will ultimately terminate in our ruin. "*Quam Deus vult perdere, prius dementat.*" The God of heaven is displeased with us, and has withdrawn from us his gracious protection. He leaves us to perish by our own wicked and foolish desires.

Our commerce becomes every day more precarious: its situation at all times, even

in

in the days of our profperity, was fubject to rifque. In ancient times the merchant traded on his own capital; but fuch has been the great increafe of navigation, that he trades now upon the capital of others. Commerce, therefore, in fome meafure, becomes a gambling adventure, depending wholly upon the fkill of the merchant in his calculation of the chances of the markets to which he fends his goods. In this he has fo much competition, that individuals frequently fuffer great loffes, and often are ruined in the conteft. Confidering this in a view of national profit, which has a regard only to the benefits accruing from the capital employed by the whole, and not by the individual, the fufferings of the latter do not appear to be of any great confequence to the public: but this is only a partial view. We fhall find, on more mature reflection, that too much of this fpirit of adventurous gambling has a dangerous effect upon the manners of a people.

At this time the national losses have fallen very heavily upon the merchants and traders; yet, in the expence of their tables, their houses, their servants, and their equipages, we see no difference. The national trade is decreased, is disordered, and is become very uncertain. The expences of the trader, on the contrary, have not decreased, but are regular and certain. As these are continued, without any apparent fund of profit from their trade to support them, we must naturally conclude, that they live merely upon the hope of the next year's being better than the last; but, at their rate of living, even this hope must at last forsake them, and ruin occupy its place.

If we take a view of the kingdom in general, we shall find that a very great proportion of its people exceed their income. By these means they contract debts, which become a heavy burden not only upon themselves, but upon the public: for the private debts of individuals have,

equally

equally with those of the public, been the only cause of both the origin and increase of the monied interest in the kingdom. This interest, as I have already taken notice, neither bears its proper share either of the labour of, or of the burdens imposed upon, the people. It is, in fact, a dead weight upon the community at large. It is true that they pay to the taxes laid upon their consumption, but this is bearing a very small part of the public burdens. They pay no taxes for their mortgages, bonds, the public funds, or other securities, of which their estates are alone composed. From these they receive an income clear of deductions.

This monied interest, which lives upon the community, is now in possession, by mortgage, of immense tracts of lands, of houses, and of vast quantities of goods and other moveables. Most of the debts, for which these securities have been given, can never be paid; the state of the kingdom will not admit it: nor is there any other possible

possible means of wiping them off than by some kind of composition. If the nation is thrown into that confusion, which is too much to be feared, this circumstance will probably happen. In times of trouble, desperate diseases are generally cured by desperate remedies. When the citizens of Rome were involved in a similar confusion, and the civil war of Rome had caused a great revolution in property, Cæsar, in his dictatorship, ordered that arbitrators should be appointed, who should value property at the rate which it sold at before the war*. — I shall conclude this subject in my next letter. — Farewel.

From on board the Britannia, at sea,
    Nov. 15, 1784.

---

* *Quum fides tota Italia esset angustior, neque creditæ pecuniæ solverentur; constituit ut arbitri darentur: per eos fierent æstimationes possessionum, et rerum, quanti quæque earum ante bellum fuissent.*
                      Cæs. *de Bello civili.*

LETTER XIV.

THE SUBJECT CONCLUDED:

THE MANNERS

OF

ROME AND LONDON

COMPARED,

AND THE

DANGER SHEWN TO WHICH THE LATTER IS EXPOSED.

Conculcari, inquam, miseram Italiam videbis.
Cic. *ad* Att.

LETTER XIV.

TO ――――――

THE prayer of Agur:—" Give me neither poverty nor riches; feed me with food convenient for me, left I be rich, and fay, Who is the Lord? or left I be poor and fteal, and take the name of the Lord in vain." This prayer ought fervently to be repeated by the British nation in this time of diftrefs, when corruption of manners has deftroyed both private and public virtue. It was the lofs of virtue which precipitated us into a war with our fellow fubjects, of which the produce alone has been poverty and difeafe of mind. The people are become poor and fteal, and take the name of the Lord in vain. They fpend the prefent hours in an expenfive and thoughtlefs manner,
wholly

wholly uncertain what the next may produce: and such are the numbers of all ranks and professions who live in this stile, keeping each other in countenance; and so familiarised are they to the want of means to supply their expences, that all sense of shame is entirely done away.

If poverty made the nation humble, if, by adversity, it had been taught wisdom, and to look forward to the fruits of industry alone, as the most certain means of restoration to wealth, it would then be a most useful monitor; but when, as in the present state of our manners, it takes away the sense of shame—when those who cannot pay in money for the luxuries which they enjoy, procure them upon trust—when the little which, perchance, is obtained, is put to the hazard at the gaming table, the common resort of such, and (I speak it with regret) of better men—when a great and general distress prevails among the whole people, there can be but one termination to it; this is public confusion.

It was a misfortune attendant upon a person, whose chief expectation arises from appointment to office, that so long as he moves within the circle of his party, he must follow both their manners and their fortune, in or out of place; for if he should quit the sphere of action, he quits all hope of provision for himself.

Were a government, on the one hand, to become so corrupt as to consider the worth or abilities of a person who fills a station under it of no avail, when put in competition with party, whether his successor be capable or not of administering the duties of office; or, on the other hand, were his own friends to live in a stile which his prudence and his virtue forbade him to follow, it must prove incumbent upon him to reflect seriously upon his condition. He must, in this examination, be convinced that he would act much more nobly in retiring from such a dishonourable and dependent situation.

I have

I have already remarked, that the former age was diftinguifhed by the poffeffion of plate, and other family riches, of great intrinfic worth. The prefent age is more remarkable for a fplendid appearance than for real and folid value. One kind of drefs is now common to almoft all ranks. The manufacturers have, therefore, accommodated themfelves to it, by making cheap fhewy filks and linens, which, inftead of being tranfmitted, as formerly, to our pofterity, is now little more than the confumption of the day.

The fame principles have operated with refpect to the more valuable ornaments, filver plate. There may be more houfes at prefent who poffefs a fideboard of plate than there were formerly; but plate itfelf is now not only made much more flight, but is frequently merely plated. The actual value, therefore, is much lefs in this age than the laft.

Befides,

Besides, there are other inconveniences attending it. A slight piece of plate diminishes from wearing much more in value than a heavy one; and as the price paid for the labour in making it is equal to the heavy price, the loss is much greater.

On the other hand, it will be said, that there is some compensation from the increased charge of the labour, the artist being a useful person in the community. The greater, therefore, the demand, the greater number of artists must be employed. Silver-plated vessels, however, which are now much used, are not compensated by even the employment of a greater number of artists. I have remarked in another place, that the silver used in this manufacture is a heavy national loss.

There are other expences common to this age, which were either unknown to the last, or happened but rarely, either to a few a few persons, or on particular occasions. These are expensive decorations in plaister, gilding, and carving of houses and carriages, as well as places of public entertainment. There is also, in our times, a much greater change in the table. Our eating formerly, though equally plentiful, was much plainer and cheaper. To these I shall add, as an intolerable grievance in the present age, the load of useless livery servants. These are a perpetual trouble, and leave no trace behind them but of wasteful expence. I cannot be understood to speak of the manner of life of the nobility and men of distinction. This was always costly, and servants are a part of their dignity. I mean the kingdom in general.

Having enlarged so much upon our expence, and our manners, I shall now attempt to describe the apparent and real fruits which, in these latter times, they have produced.

A description of our riches is a glorious, but dangerous, exhibition. The grandeur of our plate, the sparkling of our jewels, the gaudy show of our equipages, the silver decorations of our horses, the splendour of our public places, our highly-finished and costly houses, and the luxurious elegance of our tables, all proclaim the magnificence of the subjects of Britain. The bustle in our streets, the abundance of our wealth, and the taste with which it is displayed in our shops, must strike a stranger with astonishment: and should he enter into the houses of the middling sort of people, he must view with equal admiration the apparently rich sideboard of plate, the beautiful furniture, and the plentiful and expensive dishes which smoke upon the table. The whole is attended with an enjoyment of comfort unknown to other countries.

This magnificence and this appearance of comfort still remain, notwithstanding all that we have suffered: and, in point of shew, show, they even exceed thofe times in which the wealth of nations poured in upon us, and enabled us to purchafe them. Strangers, therefore, who only view the general fituation of the Englifh, pronounce them to be the richeft and happieft people in the univerfe; but thofe who have a more perfect knowledge of the country, who are acquainted with the fprings of the Government, the extent of its revenues, and the prefent actual refources of the State, find all thefe appearances to be merely fuperficial. They are made by the gentleman upon the ftrength of an eftate, the greater part of which is already feized upon by the mercilefs fangs of the monied man. They are made by the merchants and tradefmen upon the ftrength of the debts due to them upon their books, the far greater part of which will for ever remain there.

England has been a rich and happy country. She is capable of affording the higheft enjoyments: but, alas! fhe was not

not fenfible of the excellence of her condition. Like a froward child, fhe has been fpoiled by indulgence: a felf-devoted facrifice to her pride and ill humour, fhe has been herfelf the murderer of her reputation, the murderer of her peace.

Thefe are the natural confequences of luxury. Increafing the defires of a people, they make them lefs fcrupulous of obtaining them. The foldier, who had been plundered of his money, fought bravely, and received from his General praife and reward; but the recovery of his money gave him other defires than thofe which had animated him to action. The glory of his country was no longer his object; and when a poft of danger was affigned him, he replied, " General, I " have found my purfe."

This great and aftonifhing difplay of wealth recals ftrongly to our recollection the latter-days of ancient Rome. There is, however, this difference between us and

and that famous people: the character of the Romans was more sanguinary than the modern Europeans; their mode of life yet more diffolute. This fanguinary temper arofe not only from the fpirit of conqueft which familiarifed their citizens to fcenes of blood, but from their having no other attendants on their perfons, or labourers upon their lands, than flaves, which made their habits of life harfh and auftere. Their diffolute manners were occafioned by the poffeffion of vaft dominions, comprehending almoft the whole of the then known world, which contained all kinds of abundant productions that could amufe the eye, gratify the ear, or indulge the tafte. Thefe, as the inhabitants of the provinces were kept in a ftate of fevere fubjection, filled Rome with every fpecies of luxury, producing an unbounded licentioufnefs too powerful for the laws to reftrain.

Inattentive as we are to the duties which our religion inculcates, the mildnefs of
Chriftianity

Christianity has at length abolished these harsh and sanguinary customs, and has produced habits amongst us which render us less corrupt in our manners, and less cruel in our dispositions. These habits having been thus effected, slavery has been generally abolished in Europe, the rigour of war has been softened, the communication between nation and nation made easy, and our manners in general consequently more social.

I may perhaps be charged with misrepresentation when I speak of the abolition of slavery, and that this great and beneficial change in our manners has been effected by Christianity, since there are Christians who are still in the practice of this horrid custom. I can only say I am sorry that there are such. But I did not mean to misrepresent: I spoke generally of the Christians of Europe. I should feel the highest gratification could I say the same of the Christians of America.

But though the Christians of our days have arrived at a high pitch of luxury by more gentle means than the Romans, chiefly by those of commerce, yet our inordinate desires, our unbridled licentiousness, have been introduced in the same manner, and upon the same principles. The provinces from whence the luxuries of Rome were brought groaned under their government. The East Indies, from whence our luxuries have arisen, groan under a Christian, and that of a British government. The right to each is founded upon the same ground, that of conquest: not merely of conquest; there might then have been some humanity, but of ferocious conquest.

Whatever was the cause, nearly the same effects have been produced. London is now in the same situation with respect to her defence, as Rome was at the time of her fall. In describing the one, I very nearly describe the other.

In the days of her virtue every man in Rome was capable of fighting for his country. In the days of her fall, she had been so long unaccustomed to the use of arms, that she was incapable of wielding a sword in her defence: she had no army to protect her, nor any means of converting her riches into swords and spears; nor, had that been in her power, of finding, in the immense multitude of her people, men to use them.

Thus did the eternal city, the queen of nations, the mistress of the world, twice fall, within a few years, into the hands of the barbarians. Alaric and Genseric, with their savage hosts, entered the unhappy city. What escaped the Goth, in the immensity of the spoils, was plundered by the Vandal. Her citizens were massacred, were led captive, were wanderers through the earth. Those rich and powerful lords of the universe, whose senate had been compared to an assembly of kings, were now become illustrious beggars for food and raiment. The precious gems, the veffels of gold and filver, the curious pieces of art and mechanifm, the fruits of a long peace, were diffipated by barbarian hands, incapable of tafting fuch refined enjoyments. Her majeftic edifices were fhaken to their foundations.

*Barbarus heu cineres infiftet victor, et urbem
Eques fonante verberavit ungula ;
Quæque carent ventis et folibus offa quirini
(Nefas videre) diffipabit infolens* *.

The fimilarity of fituation, at leaft in many points of view, has been the caufe of my dwelling thus long upon this dreadful part of the hiftory of Rome, and of my applying thefe prophetical words of the philofophic poet to our own coun-

---

* And fell barbarians, wanton with fuccefs,
Scatter our city's flaming ruins wide,
Or thro' the ftreets in vengeful triumph ride,
And her great founders' hallowed afhes fpurn,
That fleep uninjur'd in their facred urn !
     Francis's Horace.

try.

try. I have more particularly applied it, as the remaining part of this beautiful ode relates to my next subject — that of emigration. He has predicted this destruction by the striking picture of the barbarians trampling upon her ashes, and the horsemen smiting it with the sounding hoof, insultingly dispersing those sacred monuments of her ancestors in a manner dreadful to be seen.

The recollection of the terrible effects of riots and conflagrations in the year 1780, must surely make us seriously reflect upon the danger to which the great city of London is exposed — if not to foreign and barbarous, at least to domestic and civil, commotions. The vast body of the citizens were then incapable of defending her against an unarmed banditti. The citizens of London, in our times, have acquired, by luxury, the same indolent habits into which the citizens of Rome, in her latter days, were plunged. Feebleness of mind produces feebleness of body.

body. In the year 1780, they did not appear to have the power of action. Had not the military arrived at the very inftant in which their fate feemed to be fufpended in a doubtful balance, the great and opulent city of London would moſt probably have been plundered and deſtroyed: a devaſtation which, like that of Rome, would have filled the world with horror and apprehenſion.— Farewel.

From on board the Britannia, at ſea,
    Nov. 15, 1784.

LETTER

LETTER XV.

UPON

EMIGRATION.

Cælum non animum mutant, qui trans mare currunt.

HOR.

LETTER XV.

TO ——————

In the words of the same affecting ode which I mentioned in my last letter, and which the prophetic poet addressed to his countrymen, I admonish mine of their danger. I would tell those who desire information, the way to escape the dreadful evils which await them.

Forte quod expediat, communiter, aut melior pars,
Multis carere quæritis laboribus *.*

The remedy is emigration. The road, America.

---

* But some, perhaps, to shun the rising shame,
(Which heaven approve) would by some happier
scheme ——————   *Francis's Horace.*
                                            Nulla

Nulla fic hac potior fententia *.

In the fame language I afk them, Is this a fatisfactory remedy; or, Hath any one a better to propofe? Delay not, then, to embrace the profperous gale. But,

Sic placet? An melius quis habet fuadere?
  Secunda
Ratem occupare quid moramur alite?
——————————— *eamus omnis civitas,*
Aut pars indocile melior grege: mollis et
  expes
Inominata perprimat cubilia.
Vos quibus eft virtus muliebrem tollite luctum
  Etrufca præter et volate litora †.

* There is no plan preferable to this.   *Tranf.*

† ——— Thus let the brave and wife,
Whofe fouls above th' indocile vulgar rife;
Then let the crowd, who dare not hope fuccefs,
Inglorious, thefe ill-omen'd feats poffefs:
But ye, whom virtue warns, indulge no more
Thefe female plaints, but quit this fated fhore.
            Francis's Horace.

I design to throw together some reflections upon the subject, which, in those parts that relate to the soil and climate of America, will be founded on the knowledge which I have obtained from others. When I arrive there, I shall be able to make myself practically acquainted with every necessary information. I would leave this letter till that period, were there not many people in England, who, being now very uneasy in their situation, and foreseeing great distress, are desirous of making preparations for quitting it. To these, the information which I can now give may be useful. I shall make no assertion that has not the most solid grounds to support it.

We have been lately favoured with an excellent little treatise upon the subject of emigration, from the pen of the venerable Dr. Franklin. He treats this subject with a simplicity which must make it clearly understood by the meanest reader. His intentions were to put an end to the popular delusion,

delusion, that America is a land flowing with milk and honey; in which the indulgencies of life are profusely distributed to every idle person who will be at the pains to settle there. America is really a land flowing with milk and honey; but it can only be gathered by the hand of the industrious. Emigrants must either have money of their own, or they must labour for others till they have obtained a sufficiency to settle a farm for themselves. In many parts of America the necessaries of life cost very little; and industry (hard labour is not necessary) will soon procure the comforts.

The man who brings with him sufficient money to settle a farm, does this with less pains, because he employs the poor emigrant to labour for him. The providence of God has proportioned our wants to our abilities. The voluptuousness with which the rich man has indulged himself in Europe renders him less able personally to encounter the difficulties

ties of a new settlement. The mind of the poor man being fitted to his station, bears patiently the labours which are allotted him, and works hard in the settlement, in the hope of earning money to set up for himself.

Both interest and humanity make it the universal practice of the farmers in America to treat their hired servants with kindness: they live nearly in the same manner as their masters; and there are few instances (when they happen, it is wholly owing to the idleness of the servant) in which they do not become masters themselves.

There are three principal points in view, to which the attention of those who are desirous of emigrating to America ought to be directed. These are, the situation of the state best adapted to this purpose — the occupation to be followed in it — and the adoption of some regular plan of emigration; in which the intentions, dispositions,

tions, and abilities of the perſons propoſing to form it are conſulted, connected, and well combined. I ſhall conſider theſe points diſtinctly.

It requires an examination of the ſeveral ſituations in America, to be correct in pointing out the moſt advantageous one for a ſettlement. The war has produced great alterations in that country. There are, however, general principles, which will anſwer the purpoſes that I have in view. Theſe will afford ſufficient information to thoſe perſons in Great Britain who are deſirous of emigrating to America; at leaſt, ſuch as will enable them to adopt ſome plan of aſſociation; providing in this manner, by a wiſe and timely precaution, for the proper ſeaſon when it may be neceſſary for them to put their plan in execution.

The end and deſign of emigration to America can only be the improvement of their condition. Thoſe who will chiefly emigrate

emigrate will be men of impaired or broken fortunes: amongst these there will be men of various descriptions. Those of merely useful handicraft trades may find employment in the towns. These, increasing continually in inhabitants, will be always in want of them. Those who have been merchants and traders, and who have preserved some wrecks of their fortune sufficient to induce them to make another attempt, will probably do it to advantage in the sea ports, which have grown rich and populous by the commercial spirit of their inhabitants. Others, on the contrary, will be more disposed to make settlements in the country, in some state where there is great plenty of vacant lands, where the soil is fertile, and the climate good.

I premise that I am not writing to men who have a sufficient fortune to live upon the income which it produces. These require no advice, as they may spend this income satisfactorily in almost any settled country. They may do it in London,

Newcastle, Glasgow, Liverpool, or Bristol: they may do it in Boston, New York, Philadelphia, Baltimore, or Charles Town, the great sea ports of America; and with more advantage, as these towns being in a state of increase, money may be disposed of with greater security and profit by employing it in ground rents and similar securities.

The persons in Great Britain desirous of forming a plan of emigration, to whom I desire chiefly to address myself, are those who are either masters of property sufficient to settle a tolerable estate in a new country, or such who, having no property of their own, must labour for the others in some shape or other. The latter may be divided into two classes: the one of those, who, having been labourers in their own country, must continue in that station; the other, of men of education, who must supply the want of money by industry and abilities.

I have

I have taken notice already of the employments which emigrants will find in the great towns. I have confined them merely to commerce, and useful handicraft trades. The luxury which now prevails in these towns occasioning a greater expence in living than is proper for them, will probably be made use of as an objection to this opinion. But, independently of such men receiving wages in proportion, this luxury is merely temporary, being occasioned by accidental circumstances produced by the war. The inhabitants of these places will naturally return to their primitive manners whenever these causes cease. This a short time must accomplish.

War, which is one principal cause of the present luxurious and expensive stile of living in America, is a great enemy to regularity of manners. The vicissitudes to which every country is subject in civil disputes are sudden and frequent. Scarcity and plenty are alternately produced. The government of a country in such a

situation

situation must be unequal. Whenever a temporary distress prevails, there is a necessity to make the administration rigid and severe. When these difficulties are surmounted, it becomes loose and relaxed.

When the danger is wholly at an end, a general relaxation of government and corruption of manners almost constantly take place. The first families, who act upon principle, are either ruined, or their estates greatly injured in the contest; and new men, acquiring fortune by sudden and unexpected events, rise upon their ruin. These people, who, in this manner, rise to affluence, are always profuse of money which they have gained with ease. The old families which remain (such is our natural propensity to imitate vicious manners, and even to carry them to excess, where our pride is attacked) follow their example. One cause is common to all. The distress and scarcity occasioned by the war gave place to ease and plenty at the return of peace. Mankind usually go
from

from one extreme to another. The Americans have suffered unparallelled distress. They now plunge into (I am to be understood both locally and comparatively) unparallelled luxury.

They are indebted to the French for many parts of their luxuries. Simplicity of manners in the American republics neither suited the disposition of that nation, nor afforded them the probability of preserving so powerful an influence over these new states. The French carried their views still farther. By means of dress, equipage, and the pleasures of the table, temptations which are sure to captivate young men, they endeavoured to attach the rising generation to the interests of France. There was great policy in this conduct.

The manners of an absolute government, and those of a republic, where the system of each is strictly preserved, are very opposite to each other. The honours of a Court form the manners of a kingdom; the severity of virtue, those of a republic. Luxury, therefore, may be permitted in an absolute monarchy, without injury, whilst the introduction of it into a commonwealth will terminate in its destruction. The effect which it produces in a free state is to alienate the people from the love of their country, directing their views solely to their own particular interests and pleasures. The Americans were under the highest obligations to France for her interposition in their favour; but they are not under the necessity of shewing their sense of this obligation by following the manners and customs of a kingdom unsuitable to their dispositions, and destructive to their interests.

It is very fortunate for the American republics that they have not sufficient resources within themselves to support the expence of European luxuries. There is not only a very heavy national debt due from the United States, but a confiderable one

one from the separate governments. The private debts of individuals, contracted both before and since the war, are also of magnitude. A very long space of time, and the most unremitting industry, are requisite even to reduce these burdens. To discharge them wholly, is not within the power of some of the states. Long credit in trade is an evil which will work its own cure as soon as the ill effects of it are found in the deficiencies of payment. Luxury will then, in a great measure, cease with it. There will be no money to purchase superfluities, and they will not be obtained without it.

At present, neither trade nor manners have found their proper standard. A spirit of adventure has been prevalent since the peace, which cannot fail of being ruinous. The importation of goods has been immense, and is attended with very heavy losses. It is true that these losses will only affect individuals, and that the state will be benefited; for the supplies having

having been, for many years, hazardous and uncertain, the country was in great want of goods. The introduction, therefore, of such quantities into all parts of the vast continent of America, cannot fail of advantageous effects to the people at large. But though this event will be productive of good in the end, yet the sufferings of the mercantile interest, and the blow which credit will sustain, must make it severely felt in the operation.

The effects, however, will be much less severe in these states than in the settled governments in Europe. Such rising commercial republics as the United States will recover with ease from the shock.

It may be objected to me, that I have digressed too much in the confideration of this subject; but the luxuries of the great towns in America have been represented in such a manner in Europe as to alarm those who are desirous of emigrating to the United States. Many have supposed themselves

themselves in greater danger of having their reduced fortunes wholly sunk in expences, than in receiving sufficient advantages to enable them, by industry, to repair them. I, therefore, thought this explanation necessary. — My next letter will treat of those countries which are most advantageous for a settlement. — Farewel.

From on board the Britannia, at sea,
    Nov. 20, 1784.

LETTER

LETTER XVI.

THE SUBJECT OF EMIGRATION CONTINUED;

PARTICULARLY WITH RESPECT TO SITUATION.

———

Tibur Argæo positum colona,
Sit meæ sedes utinam senectæ,
Sit modus lasso maris et viarum,
Militiæque ———
Ille terrarum mihi præter omnes,
Angulus ridet; ———
Ille te mecum locus, et beatæ
Postulant arces ———

HOR.

LETTER XVI.

TO ————————

———————————

THE following general principle may be laid down with respect to the fixing upon a situation in America for new settlements: that the farther they are removed from the sea coasts, the more profitable will be the establishment, from the superiority both of soil and climate. The coasts were first settled on account of their easy communication with Europe; but they are (those of New England alone excepted) the worst lands and the most unhealthy climate in all the states.

The interior parts of America afford the fairest prospect of advantage to settlers. These, which were increasing in a wonderful degree before the war, received a severe

severe shock from its calamities; yet a few years of peace will (it is astonishing how soon a country recovers the ravage of war) restore these ruined settlements, and fill them with a new people.

The states of New York and Pennsylvania have large tracts of fertile land, extending to the lakes, proper for the forming settlements, and very capital ones have already been made. The climate, though severely cold in winter, is very healthy; and as the inhabitants increase in number, it will in course become, by degrees, more temperate. This country will, in future, prove one of the most advantageous commercial situations in America, having, in a manner, the key of Canada, and of all the northern Indian trade. It has a direct communication with the Atlantic by the Hudson and other considerable rivers. This navigation, extending from the western sea to the lakes, has no other obstruction than by small portages, which, in time, will be converted

converted into canals. The valuable trade of furs will chiefly center in this country.

The severity of the climate in the winter, the vicinity of many tribes of Indians, who have an easy approach to this part of the country, and the certainty of its being made the principal seat of war, (should any dispute arise between the United States and Great Britain) will be the means of forming the people to habits of diligence and activity. The British, at such times, would in all probability annoy them from Canada in the same manner as the French formerly did before the war of 1756.

As nothing conduces more to the force and vigour of a nation than putting it upon its guard, and keeping it in a constant state of alarm, the inhabitants will probably be a hardy, brave, and industrious race. The country will be full of large towns and settlements, and they must be in possession of a considerable naval force upon the lakes to facilitate and

and support their great and extensive commerce.

This part, therefore, of the interior countries of these states has all the appearance of becoming the most warlike and powerful, whilst the interior parts of Virginia and the Carolinas will possess the domestic satisfactions which arise from continual peace.

These parts of Virginia and the Carolinas are the paradise of America. The climate is temperate and serene, subject neither to the excess of the summer heats nor to the severity of the winter cold. The soil fertile, full of rich and pleasant vallies, finely wooded, and watered by continual springs. The meadows produce grass for the maintenance of cattle during the winter, and the lands even bring forth, without culture, several species of grain and fruits. The different kind of game and poultry are abundant. Wine, oil, and fruits, the products of the finest countries of Europe and Asia, may be cultivated with equal facility in these happy regions. Producing an exuberance of food, they afford the equal comforts of raiment, by possessing materials from which garments of silk, cotton, and linen may, in time, as the country settles, with ease be procured.

These beautiful, extensive, and fruitful countries have, therefore, every advantage that can be derived from goodness of climate and fertility of soil. If they have not those rougher properties which form the hardy and warlike soldier, they have those infinitely-preferable qualities which constitute the quiet and peaceful citizen. Agriculture is an employment which produces the most salubrious effects both of mind and body; but there are yet objects for the most active mind. The country is finely situated for navigation. Immense bodies of water flow through it from the mountains to the western ocean; and there being

being (as I have obferved in another place) no other obftructions than fmall portages, canals will be cut, and commerce and navigation become a confiderable object.

In the inland country of Virginia and North Carolina the fettlements, in many parts, extend to the mountains. In the eaftern part of Virginia, fettlements have been made in the mountains themfelves, where fome induftrious Germans, who found the lands in the vallies taken up, have eftablifhed confiderable plantations; there is, therefore, no room for new fettlers. But in the interior parts of South Carolina, which made a very rapid increafe of inhabitants from the peace of 1762 to the late war, are yet vaft tracts of fertile lands unfettled; and it has this peculiar advantage, that although the whole of thefe countries (the more northern part in courfe approaches neareft to that of the back country of Pennfylvania) has a fine climate,

climate, yet the Carolinas being more to the south, a still higher degree of delightful temperature is to be found there.

The state of Virginia possessing lands on the other side of the mountains, and having the more immediate communication with the country on the river Ohio, many thousands have passed over them and settled themselves in that tract which lies between the mountains and the river. It is said that some emigrants have even crossed that river, and settled in the country bordering upon the lakes.

By a late settlement, the country to the southward of the Ohio is included in the state of Virginia. All the country to the northward of this great river, extending from Pennsylvania on the east, the lakes on the north, and the Mississippi on the west, are intended to be divided by Congress into ten new states—Washington, Cherfonefus, Metropotamia, Saratoga, Pesilipa,

Pefilipa, Sylvania, Michigania, Affenipi, Illinoia, and Polypotamia.

These ten ftates, fpreading over an immenfe tract of land, are traverfed by the great river Ohio in a courfe of twelve hundred miles, receiving into its waters the innumerable rivers which are fcattered over the whole country. On the north they are bounded by the five great lakes, Superior, Michigan, Huron, Erie, and Ontario, which empty themfelves into the river St. Lawrence. On the eaft they have the ftates of New York, Pennfylvania, and Virginia, whofe navigation, as well as the St. Lawrence, afford them a direct communication with the Atlantic Ocean. On the fouth they are partly bounded by the mountains; and on the weft by the vaft river Miffiffippi, whofe fource is unknown, and which, after flowing through the great continent of America, admitting into its fwelling waves the tributes of a thoufand waters, falls into the gulph of Mexico.

All

All the parts of this great country, whether by rivers which fall into the lakes on the one side, or on the other into the Ohio and Mississippi, or by those which join by small portages with the rivers of Virginia and the neighbouring states, finally connecting the Atlantic with the whole body of the western waters by means of the St. Lawrence, the Hudson, the bays of Delaware and Chesapeak, and the rivers of the Carolinas, afford a water communication unknown to any other part of the globe.

The countries which I have described, first those on this side of the mountains within the present settled states, and as these become well peopled, the lands on the Ohio were the regions which I had in view when I quoted the ode of the philosophic poet in the beginning of this letter. Referring the remaining part of this subject of emigration to my next letters, I shall now conclude by following the path which

which is there so beautifully pointed out to us, and, in his animated spirit, call out to my countrymen, " These are the fortu-
" nate plains, where the untilled land
" produces corn, and the unpruned vine
" yields its nectarious juice; where the
" fertile olive blossoms, and the purple
" fig adorns its native tree. Honey distils
" from the oaks, and the high mountains
" pour forth their waters with a murmur-
" ing rill. The friendly flocks present,
" unsought, their full udders, and wan-
" der through the luxuriant meadows un-
" molested by ravenous beasts: and many
" more things shall we, happy Englifh-
" men, view with admiration, the rainy
" winds neither injuring the grain with
" too much moisture, nor a dry soil burn-
" ing it up, a temperate climate modera-
" ting both extremes. No contagious
" distempers hurt either the inhabitants
" or their flocks, the scorching sun or
" freezing cold being alike unknown to
" these benign lands. Providence has af-
" signed

" signed to us these fortunate plains for a
" place of refuge from the vices which
" have polluted our native shores; from
" whence there shall be a happy escape
" for every good and virtuous man."

——————— arva, beata
Petamus arva, divites et insulas,
Reddit ubi Cererem tellus inarata quotannis,
Et imputata floret usque vinea:
Germinat et nunquam fallentis termes olivæ;
Suamque pulla ficus ornat arborem;
Mella cava manant ex ilice; montibus altis
Levis crepante lympha desilit pede,
Illic injussæ veniunt ad mulctra capellæ,
Refertque tenta grex amicus ubera;
Nec vespertinus circumgemit ursus ovile,
Nec intumescit alta viperis humus;
Aquosus Eurus arva radat imbribus,
Pinguia nec siccis urantus semina glebis;
Utrumque rege temperante coelitum.

Nulla nocent pecori contagia; nullius astri
Gregem æstuosa torret impotentia.
Jupiter illa pix secrevit litora genti;
Ut inquinavit aere tempus aureum;

Aere;

*Aere, dehinc ferro duravit secula; quorum
Piis secunda, vate me, datur fuga**.

Farewel.

From on board the Britannia, at sea,
    Nov. 23, 1784.

* Offering its blefsful isles and happy seats,
Where annual Ceres crowns th' uncultur'd field,
And vines, unprun'd, their blushing clusters yield;
Where olives, faithful to their season, grow,
And figs with nature's deepest purple glow.
From hollow oaks, where honey'd streams distil,
And bounds with noisy foot the pebbl'd rill;
Where goats, untaught, forsake the flow'ry vale,
And bring their swelling udders to the pail.
Nor evening bears the sheepfold growl around,
Nor mining vipers leave the tainted ground,
Nor wat'ry Eurus deluges the plain,
Nor heats excessive burn the springing grain.

O'er the glad flocks no foul contagion spreads,
Nor summer sun his burning influence sheds.
Pure and unmix'd the world's first ages roll'd;
But soon as brass had stain'd the flowing gold,
To iron harden'd by succeeding crimes,
Jove for the just preserv'd these happy climes;
To which the gods their pious race invite,
And bid me, raptur'd bard, direct their flight.
                    Francis's Horace.

LETTER XVII.

THE SUBJECT OF EMIGRATION CONTINUED:

THE EMPLOYMENTS OF EMIGRANTS IN AMERICA.

Omnium autem verum, ex quibus aliquid acquiritur, nihil est agricultura melius, nihil ubericius, nihil dulcius, nihil homine, nihil libero, dignius.

CIC. *de* OFF.

LETTER XVII.

TO ──────

My last letter was confined to an inquiry after a situation in the United States best adapted to the purposes of those who are desirous of emigrating to America, and of forming settlements in that country. The most advantageous occupations to be followed there will be my present subject.

Agriculture will be the general employment of those who emigrate to America. Industrious, sober, and attentive farmers, of knowledge in husbandry, with a little money to begin a settlement, are sure of acquiring, in a short time, large and profitable farms. The fertility of the lands gives them assurances of plentiful crops, and the temperature of the climate gives them

them affurances of health to enjoy the fruits of them.

In my general introduction to the fubject of emigration I have fpoken curforily of thofe people, who, having been merchants, traders, or ufeful handicraftfmen, for fettling in the great towns. not in a condition to give encouragement to manufacturers in general. The following are thofe who have alone a profpect of fuccefs.

All manufacturers of the coarfer parts of iron, which, from the expence and inconvenience of carriage, cannot be brought from a diftance without great difadvantage — all thofe who have a mechanical turn in the greater or more ufeful manufactures of that metal, and which bear a relation to hufbandry and other tools, and to the conftruction of mills of various kinds — builders, carpenters, joiners, mafons, bricklayers, plafterers, fmiths, glaziers, plumbers, and fimilar ufeful trades

— handi-

—handicraftsmen, such as shoemakers, taylors, and such kind of people — manufacturers of linen from Scotland or Ireland, also of coarse cotton, may, in general, if they are sober, ingenious men, practically and well versed in their occupations, depend upon encouragement.

On the contrary, clothiers, silk and other weavers, Birmingham and Sheffield toy manufacturers, jewellers, coach-makers, and every other species of manufacturers which depends upon luxury, will find no employment. The present rage for luxury in the great towns may hold out a delusive encouragement; but this will be for the reason which I have already given, merely temporary. When this evil (which I have already observed will cure itself, for the want of money to purchase European luxuries) is at an end, the emigrants of this species, who have found employment, must become labourers. This, however, will be an advantage, as labourers in America

rica are well clothed, and their labour abundantly paid.

But although the first species of manufacturers which I have described will, in general, find advantageous employments to themselves, and may be rendered very useful during their residence in the towns, yet such are the peculiar advantages attending agriculture, not only in the acquisition of a stock of money, but in the acquisition of a stock of health, that there are very few who have procured money sufficient to make a settlement that will not prefer this mode of life to any other employment.

This will, therefore, produce beneficial effects. It will be a perpetual fund of advantage both to the American States and to persons of those occupations who are desirous of emigrating to them. New settlements in the country will be continually forming by those, who, having acquired knowledge by their residence in the States, may be assured of immediate success, lea-

ving

ving their occupations to similar manufacturers and tradesmen who emigrate to America. By these means the country will receive a constant increase of new inhabitants, and a profitable succession of people be kept up in the towns.

Men of useful, rather than critical, literature, of sound, rather than subtile, understandings, and of sincere, rather than refined, manners, to superintend the education of children, will find ample encouragement. America, especially the interior parts, is in great want of such characters. She has several seminaries of education, though by no means equal to the extent of the country. In these are many professors of extensive learning, and of comprehensive minds. Men of clear and sound understanding, and of acute and solid judgement, are, in general, much more frequently to be met with in America than in almost any other nation. Their writings do honour to the most finished stile.

Agriculture

Agriculture muſt then be conſidered by thoſe who emigrate, as the firſt, all others as only ſecondary employments. But it is indiſpenſably requiſite to ſucceſs, that the emigrant be active and induſtrious. He muſt work in ſome ſhape or other, either by his head or his hands. The neceſſaries, the comforts, and the indulgences of life, may be procured by labour; but even the neceſſaries are not to be procured without it. America ſupports very fully the propriety of the proverb, " Idleneſs is the " parent of want, and of pain." No people are more ready to aſſiſt the ſtranger than the back ſettlers; but they expect to find in others the ſame activity and induſtry with which their own endeavours are exerted.

It would be an infringement of the rules of ſocial induſtry, a quality abſolutely neceſſary to the exiſtence of new ſettlements, were not this to be conſidered as an inviolable law. In ſuch countries, indolence is an evil which effects its own puniſhment,

ment, and muſt work out its own cure. The cup is within the reach of every man, full to the brim; but the exertion to take it muſt ariſe from himſelf. So long as he has the capacity, he cannot, and he ought not, to receive it from any other hand.

I have frequently made uſe of the term, indulgencies of life. I think an explanation neceſſary, leſt I ſhould be underſtood to mean its delicacies. No fanciful ornaments are here to be met with to adorn the perſon, or the high-flavoured ſauces of a French cook to pamper the body. It would be a wiſe conduct in thoſe who have been accuſtomed to this kind of life, and who are under the neceſſity of emigrating to America, to endeavour to find out ſome ſpot in Scotland or Ireland, where the manners of our forefathers are yet preſerved, and where all that is conſumed in the family is produced within its domain. In this manner will both food and raiment be procured in the part of America which I have been deſcribing.

The climate of Great Britain bestows upon its inhabitants few of the indulgencies, and is often parsimonious of the necessaries of life. The climate of these parts of America not only grants to the people necessaries, but even indulgencies in abundance. Wine, beer, cyder, oil, will be produced in great plenty. Butcher's meat of all kinds, and every species of poultry and game, in excess. The mildness of the winter, the richness of the pasture, and the fertility of the corn lands, cause this great exuberance of provisions. Food is, therefore, obtained with great ease. Our next care is raiment.

This, or the chief part of it, must be manufactured in the family. The country supplies sufficient materials. I once saw in a family of distinction in Scotland, both woollen and linen cloth manufactured within the house, which were of a perfectly good quality. A great number of the emigrants to America are Irish and Scotch

Scotch manufacturers. These have been usefully employed already, in manufacturing linen in America. But America, like the East, supplies an equally, if not more pleasant manufacture, that of cotton. Of this there is plenty, which has been long in use, not only in the back countries, but in some of the settled parts on the coast. South Carolina, many years ago, when she was disappointed of her usual supply of woollen cloth from England, on account of the war, manufactured a sufficient quantity of cotton for her negroes.

The fashion is as immaterial as the texture; the less complex, the more pleasant to the wearer. The Roman form of dress had a much greater simplicity than those of the present inhabitants of Europe, whose customs originally sprung from our savage ancestors, the barbarous nations of the north. All the clothes, which were worn by many eminent Romans, were the produce of their own families. The

Emperor Auguſtus never made uſe of any other. Such examples, given at a time when the Romans had attained to the heighth of their power, proves that they were not ſingular. The luxury after this period, indeed, had no bounds ſet to it, but ended in the common ruin which ſpread through Rome and Italy. But the proof that this practice did exiſt amongſt the firſt people, is ſufficient to ſhew the facility of its execution, and, I am ſure, with much greater comfort; for we have the luxury of linen, to which the Romans were ſtrangers.

The furniture of our houſes becomes our next conſideration. The ſimplicity of our lives in theſe ſequeſtered ſpots will make the fine linens, the rich ſilks, and the coſtly furniture of Europe, unneceſſary and uſeleſs. Inſtead of admiring the works of art, we muſt content ourſelves with admiring the works of nature. Some of the vegetable productions produce both

food

food and raiment, whilſt others preſent themſelves to the joiner, to be formed into plain and uſeful furniture for our habitations. In many parts, the earth yields iron for the harder purpoſes of providing food. In others, clays, which may be moulded into ſweet and wholeſome veſſels, made upon the ſpot, in useful ſhapes. We have only to ſtudy convenience and neatneſs; the comforts of life will follow, and amply ſupply the want of elegance and ſplendour.

The picture which ſome late writers have drawn of the miſerable ſtate of the emigrants, is truly ridiculous.

Thoſe who are deſirous of emigrating to America, and have no money to pay for their paſſage, endeavour to make an agreement with a maſter of a ſhip bound to that country. The maſter muſt be ſatisfied for the paſſage; the emigrants have no money to pay him: they, therefore,

agree

agree to indent themselves servants for a term, generally for four years, which is to make satisfaction to the master for the passage. Upon their arrival in America, it is necessary to find some method to exchange this indenture for money, or the master of the ship will receive no benefit. This can only be done by the emigrants engaging with some of the inhabitants of the country, to serve them as labourers during the term of years for which they have been indented; and this in consideration of certain sums of money, which they have agreed shall be paid to the master of the vessel as a compensation for the passage that he has given them.

Great numbers of indented servants have emigrated this year from Ireland, whose servitude is thus disposed of:—They are treated with humanity and tenderness, have the same food as their masters, and are plentifully supplied with the necessaries and comforts of life. If they have industry,

industry, and give satisfaction to their masters, they cannot fail of procuring a settlement for themselves.

There is also another species of emigrants who go from Ireland. These are substantial farmers and householders, who, with their families, have, this year, to the amount of several thousands, already sailed from Londonderry, Newry, and Belfast. They have not only sufficient property to pay for their passage, but are able to raise a considerable sum in money amongst themselves, which they carry with them. This they generally dispose of in forming settlements in the interior parts of America. Instances may be given where a whole parish in Ireland has emigrated in this manner, possessed of considerable property.

In a country where the inhabitants have a temperate climate, and preserve regularity of manners, they are in possession,

sion, as a natural consequence, of health and chearfulness. The family retire early to rest, and awake early to labour. The diligence of the master is attended with success, which softens fatigue, and excites emulation. It is by such means that the wilds of America have been turned into beautiful pastures, and filled with inhabitants.

In such happy climes, the natural distribution of time, and distinction of employments, have each their just and proper functions assigned them. The irregular customs of England are unknown here. Night is not turned into day, nor day into night. The morning will not be devoured by sleep, nor shall we lounge at breakfast till one o'clock, dine at five or six, or amuse ourselves at Ranelagh till two or three in the morning. These are the enjoyments which we leave behind us in Europe. Instead of carrying with us such wretched habits, let ours be more rational

rational purfuits, and let us fay with Fabius Maximus, *Deos iratos Tarentinis relinquemus*— We will leave to the Tarentines their angry gods.— I fhall continue this fubject in my next letter.— Farewel.

From on board the Britannia, at fea, Nov. 25, 1784.

LETTER

LETTER XVIII.

THE SUBJECT OF EMIGRATION CONTINUED;

UPON THOSE PERSONS ABOUT THE COURT WHO WILL PROBABLY LEAVE ENGLAND.

Quisnam igitur liber ? Sapiens, sibique imperiosus
Quem neque pauperies, neque mors, neque vincula terrent,
Reponsere cupidinibus contemnere honores
Fortis ———

          Hor.

THE laſt in order, but the firſt in conſequence, is the proper arrangement of a regular plan of emigration. In this plan a combination ſhould be formed of perſons diſpoſed in ſuch adequate proportions, by the diſtribution of rank, property, and abilities, as to render them mutually aſſiſtant to each other. It is a prudent conduct, even in thoſe who change their abode from one ſettled country to another, to be previouſly made known to ſome of the inhabitants with whom they are in future to reſide. How much more neceſſary, therefore, is it for men who emigrate to a new country, where ſuch an opportunity of introduction is not to be procured, to be cautious how they proceed!

Many

Many difficulties muſt naturally occur to a ſingle perſon, which, to a number, could ſcarcely bear that name. Our attention ought, therefore, chiefly to be directed to the forming a proper ſociety; for it is not the clods of earth of which our country is compoſed, but the friends with whom we live, and to whom we are attached by mutual good offices, which engage our affection and regard. But before I enter upon the nature of the plan which I have mentioned, I ſhall take into the view the ſeveral ranks and orders of men in Great Britain whoſe intereſt or inclination leads them to emigrate to America.

My attention will be firſt directed to thoſe perſons who poſſeſs, or who are candidates for employments under the Crown, and who live within the circle of the Court, whether they are men of birth and diſtinction, or have riſen to rank by their abilities.

There are, amongst these, persons of the first rank, who do honour to the dignity they possess; and there are amongst their connections men who have too much spirit to submit to any yoke, when a free country opens its arms to receive them. There are others, on the contrary, of equal rank, or who live within the circle of the Court, who are less scrupulous. Of the latter I shall now speak.

These are either men of fashion, who have no other ground or principle of action than what arises from the most disagreeable qualities of the human mind, or persons of distinction, in whom self interest produces equally bad effects, though by different means. The latter are mere machines, guided by avarice or ambition. The former are the butterflies of the day, whose empty joys are confined to a taste for dress or equipage, who are distinguished by either the act of embellishing their gilded houses, of decorating their elegant tables, or of shewing the excellence of their palate,

palate, by producing dishes of the most exquisite relish. Such men, to whatever party they belong, ought merely to be considered as the ornamental lumber of the palace; the property of every prince who possesses it. These, therefore, can have no part in considerations upon the subject of emigration.

I come now to speak of men of birth and distinction, possessed of great landed property, and of high desert. If these submit to unjustifiable measures, their minds must be either degraded to their situation, or they must have in contemplation an emigration to another country with the shattered remains of such part of their fortunes as they can gather from their estates. When vast landed property is obliged to be exposed to sale, there are very few purchasers to be met with; and, in general, settlements and intails are obstacles to the sale of most of the great English estates.

The condition of perfons in this fituation, as well of men who have rifen to rank merely by their abilities, without the advantages of birth or fortune, differs in this circumftance — the former poffefs the election of living a private life in their own country, by fubmitting to its government — the latter are deprived of it for the want of fufficient property to fupport their rank. I fuppofe them to be equally men of principle, incapable of proftituting themfelves, or their talents, to the fupport of any corrupt government.

The making of an election by a perfon to leave his country, who has not the means of continuing in it with honour to himfelf, is foftened in fome degree by its neceffity: but to make an election, in which a man of birth and diftinction, long ufed to habits of deference to his perfon, and indulgence of his defires, furrenders up the means which procured them, is fo fevere a trial of his fortitude, as to become an act of exalted virtue. Such

Such instances are rare; but they may be found even in this degenerate age.

Want of riches in a republic is not attended with the reproach which it bears in a monarchical state. In England, the road to honour, preferment, and the accumulation of wealth, is open to every man of talents in public life: but if the attainment of wealth be attended with lofs of principle, and a man of abilies rejects them with disdain — if contentedly, viewing

———————— *paternum*
Splendet in menfa tenui fal***m *,

He lives with ———— ——— the little mo-
————   ———, poffiffes, he will be a
————— — free state. Men, who are
capable of facrificing their interests to their

---
* ———— whose frugal board,
His father's plenty can afford.
      Francis's Horace.

integrity,

integrity, must ever be a valuable acquisition to the country which receives them.

I have said there are amongst the connections of men of rank and distinction, living within the circle of a Court, many men, who have too much spirit to submit to a yoke, when a free country opens its arms to receive them. I am very desirous of taking the state of such men into particular consideration.

I do not mean the generality of the persons employed in the public offices. These have, in a manner, been educated in the school of obedience, and have no will but that of the masters whom they serve. When a new ministerial system of government was reduced into practice, and the Whigs were turned out of place, all their connections, to the lowest clerks in office, were discharged from their employments. But when it was discovered that this violence would not gain the point aimed at, without a severe contest, and that the means exifted of obtaining it in a much lefs difficult manner, this practice ceafed.

Since that period clerks in office have been ftationary. Obedience to their principal, or rather to the fecretary or deputy who is fet as a watch over them, is alone required. There is generally in the public offices fome ftationary fecretary, or chief clerk, who directs the bufinefs of it.

I have faid thus much upon this fubject, in order to prevent any confufion that might arife from the blending of characters. The mere clerks in office may therefore be added to the fame lumber (though not fo ornamental) which belongs to whatever prince poffeffes the palace. The perfons whofe fituation I wifh to take into particular confideration are the confidential friends of men of rank and diftinction, who follow their fortunes, and who come in or go out of place with the party with whom they are connected.

Public

Public business cannot be carried on to advantage in any country, where those persons who are most capable of forming the executive part of government are subject to be displaced whenever a party prevails; nor, on the contrary, can any man of principle remain in office when no other ground of action is suffered than that of passive obedience. We have seen, by experience, that the manner in which a person is required to conduct himself in this situation will infallibly disgrace them.

A genuine Whig cannot be dependent upon any principal or party, whose opinions do not coincide with his own. In lesser points, for all men of the same party cannot be brought to an union of sentiment, it is his duty to submit his opinions to his superiors; but, in all measures of importance, he has no such duty to fulfil: he is to be guided by his own unbiassed judgement; and he is answerable to God alone for the proper employment of the faculties

faculties which, in his providence, he has bestowed upon him.

Granting the existence of such a state, it must naturally follow that public business cannot be carried on to the greatest advantage; neither can any of those persons, whom I particularly allude to, amongst the Whig connections, (however qualified for it) remain in place. Such men cannot undergo the humiliating condition of becoming, like the stationary men in office, the mere instruments of obedience.

There are other difficulties which such persons labour under, even amongst their own connections. A person of this description may enjoy the full confidence of a leading member in the government: he may enjoy the friendship of the minister himself, and have not only free access to his person, but to other parts of administration; all of whom may have a good opinion of his parts and integrity. He may

may be attentive and active in the bufinefs of his office: he may eftablifh in it great and material reforms, and be otherwife employed in important public affairs: farther, as he, in a manner, lives amidft the members of adminiftration, he neceffarily becomes acquainted with almoft every public tranfaction: yet, a perfon with all thefe capital advantages, and whofe fituation is the object of envy and refpect, muft poffefs other lefs eftimable qualifications before he can fucceed in any profitable views for himfelf or his family.

His ill fuccefs arifes from the voluptuoufnefs of manners which pervades almoft every corner of England, efpecially the principal families. The fashionable vices of gaming and high living are become, by this means, fo very prevalent, that a fimilarity of manners can only fecure the friendfhip of thofe in whofe hands are the iffues of lucrative employments. Good dinners are an excellent, and the moft certain, road to preferment.

I am sensible that there are many persons of the first distinction in England, who are wholly free from these views: but this singular moderation of conduct, in men of rank and family, is generally connected with mildness of disposition and ease of temper. These qualities continually subject them to be overborne by men who, having bolder features in their character, not only set the world at defiance in private life, but assume the lead in all matters of party. It may happen that such a person is connected with a man who has risen to rank by his abilities alone: but although those abilities have commanded a high situation for himself, such is the jealousy entertained of great talents which have not the fortuitous assistance of birth and riches to support them, that they are not suffered (quitting the common routine of office) to be exerted by the selection of proper persons, however adapted their capacities may be for particular employments.

Besides,

Besides, although the Whig leaders are faithful stewards for the public, they are most miserable patrons. They are themselves practised in the virtues of integrity and disinterestedness to an eminent degree. In a private capacity, they are kind, indulgent, and affectionate. Their purses, whenever it is in their power, are open to reward and relieve — their time chearfully employed to comfort and assist their friends. Yet even a knowledge of circumstances, which, in a private situation, would have a full and immediate effect upon their affections, has no manner of influence when the desired reward for service is to proceed from the public purse.

But although they are thus callous, almost to the entire neglect of their friends, the public receives no benefit; for these very rewards are often suffered to be enjoyed by those who are not only without attachment, but who are very frequently inimical to them. This conduct arises from no other motive than the fear of

being

being accufed of partiality in the diftribution of employments.

I may, perhaps, be fuppofed by many to have dwelt too long upon this fubject; but I had not only in view the particular fituation of the perfons whom I have defcribed, but I was defirous of explaining fome circumftances which are ill underftood by the public with refpect to the perfons themfelves. Their fituation in England is very precarious. Should there be a change of adminiftration, they muft know, by experience, that they have no profpect of enjoying fufficient emoluments to admit even thofe common fatisfactions, which, in their rank of life, they have reafon to expect. If this event fhould not take place, they have a certainty of ftill more grievous difappointment.

The propriety, therefore, of fuch perfons removing from a country where they have little to expect, and much to fear, to fettle in a rifing ftate, where, on the contrary,

trary, their hopes greatly exceed their apprehenfions, feems not to admit of doubt. So long as the prefent fyftem remains in England, there will be an uneafy dependence, which obtains not only in fuch perfons whom I have mentioned, but in every perfon whatever belonging to adminiftration, even to the minifter himfelf; fo long, therefore, will the fituation of perfons dependent upon a Court be rendered weary and troublefome. — My fubject increafes upon me fo much, that I muft refer the confideration of the fituation of thofe perfons who will probably emigrate to America to another letter. — Farewel.

From on board the Britannia, at fea,
Nov. 27, 1784.

LETTER

LETTER XIX.

THE SUBJECT OF EMIGRATION CONTINUED.

UPON THE DIFFERENT RANKS OF PEOPLE WHO WILL PROBABLY LEAVE ENGLAND.

Incipe cum paupertate habere commercium.
Aude, Hospes, contemnere opes, et te quoque dignum
Finge Deo ———

Nemo alius est Deo dignus, quam qui opes contempsit. Quarum possessione tibi non enterdico; sed efficere volo, ut illas intrepide possideas. Quod uno consequeris modo, si te etiam sine illis beatè victurum persuaseris tibi; si illas tanquam exituras semper adspexeris.
SENECA.

LETTER XIX.

TO ──────

I SHALL now quit the Court for the city, and inquire into the state of those who will most probably emigrate from it. In the observations which I have made upon the manners of this age, I have remarked the expensive life of the people in general. Amongst these are the far greater part of the merchants and tradesmen; which, combined with the general complaints of the decay of trade, and the want of money, naturally leads us to reflect upon the end of such unusual and dangerous appearances. I do not think it necessary to examine into the means by which this expence is supported. This I know to be precarious. I merely recommend

mend an inquiry how long they will probably laſt.

It will be found, on this inquiry being made, that the countenance of this manner of life in the city will laſt ſo long as the credit of the mercantile intereſt is preſerved, and that it muſt ceaſe with the firſt violent blow which that intereſt receives. We know that the debts which appear on the different books, firſt, of the merchants who ſhip goods—next, on thoſe of the great tradeſmen who ſell for export—and laſtly, of the ſhopkeepers of the metropolis in general, conſtitute the bulk of the property, upon the ſtrength of which theſe heavy expences are ſupported. We alſo know, that there is every reaſon to expect a ſtill greater increaſe of the grievances which are the ſubject of complaint. It amounts, therefore, to a demonſtration, that it is every day drawing nearer and nearer to an end.

I have

I have already shewn that we ought not to place a dependence either upon the payment of the former debt due from the citizens of America, or the more recent engagements which have been entered into for the goods exported to thofe States fince the peace. The country has been too much reduced, by the war that Great Britain waged againft her, to be in the capacity of difcharging them. As little reafon have we to expect the folvency of the Eaft-India Company, in whofe fate the city is fo deeply involved. Thefe two events will be amongft the calamitous blows which the commercial intereft will receive, and by which their particular grievances will be increafed.

The landed intereft has been alfo fhewn to have its full fhare of the evils to which the country, in its prefent ftate, is fubject, and therefore equally incapable of fuftaining the burden of its debts. The payments at prefent are fo partially made, that a general ceffation does not appear to be be very far diſtant. The intereſt of money, ariſing from the immenſe mortgages with which this intereſt is incumbered, and which muſt be paid, is collected at this time by the mortgagee with great difficulty. We are drawing near to the criſis to which all countries immerſed in luxury, and burdened with taxes, are ſubject: a criſis too often accompanied by a revolution fatal to its liberty.

A ſtile of living, maintained wholly upon credit, and ſubſiſted merely upon hope, cannot therefore be laſting; and ſuch is the chain which binds ſociety to each other, that when a ſingle link fails, the whole is broken. When the debtor is become incapable of payment, the tradeſman who truſted him is reduced to the ſame incapacity; the debt being an imaginary ſubſtance, to be found only in books.

In ſuch a ſtate there is no tolerable remedy for a ruined Engliſhman to avoid
diſtreſs

distress than to consolidate the broken wrecks of his fortune, and form a settlement in America. The man who has lived in splendour cannot descend to mean employments at home; the witnesses of his former prosperity are offensive to his feelings: he exchanges, with pleasure, the scene of his misfortunes for a settlement in a distant country, where he can again begin the world with new hopes and expectations.

The same grievances equally exist in the country as in the city; chiefly amongst the manufacturers, (who have supplied the orders for America) the merchants, bankers, and capital tradesmen. As few payments will be made to the manufacturers for the goods which they have already sold, farther orders cannot be executed. In consequence, great numbers of the workmen must be discharged for want of employment. This will be a common evil to the whole country, in which every one will bear his share.

The inhabitants of the country depend, in some measure, upon each other. Persons who retire from business generally invest their money either in mortgages or the public funds, or in lending money at interest to those who remain in trade. The inferior tradesmen, and the workmen in the different fabrics, rely solely upon the merchants and manufacturers for employment. When, therefore, the decay of trade becomes so great, that the commercial interest in London is unable to resist the torrent, their country connections will fall with them; in which case, all the inhabitants whom I have mentioned must be involved in one common fate.

As a greater sobriety of manners prevails in the country, the sufferings of the people will be less severe than those of the capital. It might, therefore, be expected that the emigration from thence would not be so considerable; but there is one cause which will operate in favour of emigration. The inhabitants are of very diligent

ligent habits, and much difposed to induftry. Thefe, finding no means in Great Britain capable of extricating them from their difficulties, will be naturally led to emigrate to a country from whence they already derive the moft promifing expectations.

The farmers, the moft valuable of the whole body of the emigrators, fill up the rear of this long lift. Thefe, having fhared in the general profperity which refulted from the peace of 1762, followed the example of their neighbours, indulging themfelves with many fuperfluities, to which they had before been ftrangers. Agriculture being then a profitable occupation, the farmers had an opportunity of raifing a capital of their own. With this money they were enabled to bid againft each other for farms, many of which were confolidated by the landlords, and the rents advanced, as faft as the leafes fell in. By thefe means eftates, in general, were

were greatly raised in value through the kingdom.

So long as the national prosperity continued, these rents were not only punctually paid, but the lands, in general, improved. The country being, however, now fallen into a state of decay, the farmers are become incapable of continuing the same rents. They have not only sacrificed the little property which they had accumulated, but are now so much in debt, that they have no other means of fully satisfying their landlords than by surrendering their stock in payment. This many of them have already been obliged to do, and to quit their farms.

There are few estates where the rents are not at this time greatly in arrear. The farmers, therefore, in general, find such difficulty in living upon their farms, even in the most frugal manner, that many have already expressed a strong desire to emigrate to America. They want only

only the means to put it in practice. This disposition is not confined to the common farmers, who have only a lease of lands: it is extended to a large body, who have small estates of their own, which they cultivate themselves. These, finding similar difficulties, have an equally strong inclination to emigrate. A difficulty in the disposal of their estates forms the chief obstruction to their desire. They would each of them, in their different stations, be useful subjects. The one would be found industrious masters; the other diligent labourers.

I have now, as I originally designed, gone through the several ranks of men in Great Britain whose inclination or interest leads them to emigrate to America. I except the common people alone, who must follow the fate of those who will give them employment, either at home or abroad. It is evident that there are great numbers of people, who are either desirous, or who will be obliged by necessity to emigrate to America; some in tolerable circumstances, some without any property at all: many who make amends for the want of property by their abilities; others by activity: two very essential qualities to the well-being of a new settlement. In short, there are few people, who, if they have good dispositions, may not be rendered useful to each other in a plan of emigration, composed of persons judiciously combined together.

Many advantages arise from such associations. Emigration is at all times attended with some difficulties, especially to those who embark singly, or even in small parties, without the necessary precaution of forming a regular plan of society for the purpose. The settlement of an association upon a consistent and extensive plan prevents these embarrassments. Those who compose such a society, becoming previously acquainted with each other, are enabled to fix upon the necessary arrangements with ease and satisfaction.

An

An association, formed upon the systematic plan of founding a considerable settlement, should comprehend within it all the views necessary for its establishment and prosperity. Every member ought to have his post assigned him. Some of them should be sent over to lay the foundation of a new settlement. Others should be fixed in the nearest American seaports to receive the emigrants which are sent from the society to strengthen the settlement, as well as the other supplies necessary for its improvement and success; whilst another part of the association (constantly receiving an accession of new members) ought to remain at home, to send out supplies, and to dispose of any returns of merchandize which the settlers might find for their advantage to send them: in short, to superintend the affairs of the society in general, or of those of any particular member in it, who should have occasion for their assistance.

In the arrangements of the different parts of the affociation, regard fhould be paid to the properly contrafting the perfons who find money with thofe who have only labour to offer, that the whole may be rendered ufeful to each other. Many members may have abilities adequate to the direction and management of the whole, or of different parts of the undertaking, and yet not be poffeffed of property: other members may have property, without thefe neceffary abilities. The labour of the one, and the property of the other, muft be made fubfervient to each other in fuch a manner as to promote the general good of the whole.

Thofe who have the greateft knowledge of America ought to be fent out to examine the country, and to fix upon a proper fituation to eftablifh the fettlement. When this is determined upon, a part of the affociation muft be felected for the purpofe of forming it, attended by ufeful handicraftfmen and labourers, and equipped with

with tools and all other neceſſaries for a plantation. The members who, as I have already remarked, ſhould be fixed in the neareſt American ſeaport, might be previouſly diſpatched in order to receive them.

This embarkation of ſettlers ſhould be choſen from thoſe who have abilities, whether they have property or not, as the firſt eſtabliſhment is attended with the greateſt difficulties, and requires both a ſolid judgement to plan, and an operative vigour to execute. Beſides, if there are a ſufficient number of members who have abilities, without property, it is reaſonable that, as the forming the ſettlement is the moſt difficult part, they ſhould be made choice of for the firſt expedition. That thoſe who find money ſhould alſo find an eſtabliſhment provided for them againſt their arrival. The indented ſervants will in courſe be provided for in the uſual manner: but a portion of land ought to be aſſigned to them at the end of their terms of ſervitude.

All manner of useful handicraftsmen must form a part of the undertaking. Capenters, masons, smiths, and every other trade that bears any relation to agriculture or building. When the settlement is so much increased as to stand in need of superior mechanical professions, as engineers, millwrights, or builders, such persons will easily be induced to join the association, from the ample encouragement which they would be certain to receive.

A few observations upon the first expeditions to America, and upon the assent of the Government to emigrations at this time, will conclude the subject. I shall refer them to my next letter, and now bid you farewel.

From on board the Britannia, at sea,
    Nov. 30, 1784.

LETTER XX.

THE SUBJECT OF EMIGRATION CONTINUED;

THE SITUATION OF THE FIRST AND PRESENT SETTLERS OF AMERICA CONTRASTED;

AND THE WHOLE CONCLUDED,

Non ignara mali, miseris succurrere disco.
                                        VIRG.

LETTER XX.

TO ——————

ALL the American colonies were founded upon similar institutions. It may probably be objected to me, that very few of the first settlers were succesful: they were chiefly destroyed either by famine or disease, or by the arrows of the Indians, whose territories they usurped. The illustrious Penn, the first and most humane of lawgivers, is the only exception amidst the various settlements of the great continent of the western world. It is necessary, in order to remove these objections, to inquire into the cause of this ill success.

The whole country was at that time a wilderness, the few inhabitants in it hostile, and the climate, particularly on the

sea

sea coast, (where the settlers were obliged to establish themselves) very indifferent. A variety of causes reduced them to the necessity of making this choice. Their possessions were narrow, and circumscribed —the spot upon which they landed was their whole estate; for the title to which they were indebted alone to the superiority of their arms. A proximity to the sea, from whence they came, was therefore necessary to their safety, that they might be open to supplies from the mother country; without which they could not have expected long to subsist.

The event shewed the wisdom of this choice. It proved the only means by which the surviving settlers were preserved amidst the distress and disorder of their first establishment. Many perished. The distance from the mother country, and the civil commotions which reigned in it, soon after the first settlement of America, preventing general relief, some settlements were wholly ruined and broken up, the inhabitants

inhabitants dying of difeafe and want of food. Thofe who remained were indebted for their prefervation to the partial fupplies which they received, abating, in fome degree, the daily and fevere trials which thefe poor people endured, and which they bore with exemplary patience and refignation. This fpirit of perfeverance, joined to the activity and induftry which the firft fettlers poffeffed, and which their defcendants have inherited from them, have been the caufe of their great and wonderful increafe.

Thus was America fituated in the time of the firft fettlers of that country. The ftate in which emigrants will now find it forms a very ftrong contraft. The New England, and the fea coafts of all the other ftates, are well fettled, and full of people. Even the back countries of the middle and fouthern ftates I have fhewn to be filled with great and profitable farms, extending, in many parts, to the mountains, feveral hundred miles from the fea.

In

In the midst of these countries are large and populous towns. On the coasts are great and powerful cities.

Instead, therefore, of labouring under disease and want, from not receiving supplies from the mother country; instead of being under the necessity of forming establishments in the midst of enemies, the present emigrants will now settle in the midst of friends, speaking their own language, and following their own customs — in the midst of towns, where, in case of want, they may purchase all the necessary instruments for planting — in a plentiful country, where they will find food in abundance — in a temperate climate, where the few garments they want may be procured with ease and chearfulness.

They also receive another great advantage by the assistance of the farmers of the country, in the forming of their settlements. These, from the natural desire of augmenting

augmenting the number of their neighbours, are ſtimulated to render every facility in their power to new comers. The whole country has been thus formed out of the wildernefs. Settlers have affifted each other in clearing thofe fertile regions, till they have at length reached the mountains, from whence there is now either a fleet of boats on the water, or a ſtring of waggons on the road, loaded with the fruits of their labours. Thefe they carry for fale to the fea ports. As the country increafes in inhabitants, the farms increafe in value. The encouragement, therefore, which they afford to new fettlers by their affiftance, is rewarded by the benefits which their eftates derive from this increafe of people.

There are, doubtlefs, many perfons in Great Britain who will think the picture which I have drawn of the ſtate of that country fomewhat overcharged. I have taken fo decided a part myfelf, that I muft be fuppofed to write from conviction:

but even allowing, for the fake of argument, that I have been mistaken in some points, it is impossible that even such persons can be wholly free from apprehension. The question, therefore, that ought to weigh with them is, whether it would not be prudent to make some provision against an event of magnitude, which cannot possibly amend their circumstances in any great degree, yet may produce to them ruinous consequences? They would not, in such a case, pursue a conduct that would more conduce to prepare them for the event, than by embarking in the plan of association which I have described. It would not carry them to America per force. They would have the opportunity of remaining at home, and superintending the society, till the national affairs were brought to such a crisis as would enable them to make an election.

Such persons would then reap the very capital advantage of possessing property in both countries. By this means they would.

would be always assured of some place of security. If the affairs of Great Britain took such a dangerous turn as to render it a matter of too great hazard to remain in it, the settlement of the association in America would be ready to receive them. If they took a favourable turn, their property in America (if the settlement was judiciously made) would make them a return of profit manifold. In every case they would be the gainers. In one situation, this conduct would prove their preservation: in both, it would be increasing their wealth.

I shall, perhaps, be asked for the authority upon which I have grounded my assurances of the practical execution of this plan in Great Britain? and whether it is probable that the Government will suffer such an association to take place?

To the last of these questions I shall answer, without hesitation, Yes: and I shall then give the following reasons in support of the authority upon which I ground these assurances:

I do not conceive that any Administration would venture to lay any restraint upon emigration; but when a great number of people, oppressed with taxes, either reduced to beggary for want of employment, or their property wasting in such a manner as to make them daily apprehensive of this misfortune — when such persons, I say, have an asylum held out to them, in which they see a clear and certain prospect of the restoration of their affairs, is it probable that they would not, by some means, evade an obedience to a government which could impose such a restriction upon their natural rights?

The prince of any country would indeed be very ill advised, should he retain in his dominions, by force, a number of hostile subjects, if, full of resentment to his ministers, they considered them as the cause of all their calamities. It would be be adding infult to infult to deny them the liberty of retiring in peace, the only method in which they might be defirous of expreffing their fenfe of the injuries which had been done to them.

I have now to defire both your pardon and indulgence. The one, for any matter in thefe letters which takes up unneceffarily your time: the other, for the errors which may have involuntarily flipped from me. For the firft I have no other excufe than what your kindnefs will fuggeft for me: for the laft I have to plead the inconveniencies of a voyage, and the want of thofe references which are ufeful in many parts of fuch a work as this. If I have miftaken any circumftance, I am wholly unconfcious of it. I have taken pains to avoid it, and I believe I have been correct.

I am now arrived at the laft ftage of the journey which I have undertaken. It has been hitherto performed with many a weary

weary and painful step, very much resembling my own journey of life. The beginning of that journey was indeed prosperous; for I entered the world full of gaiety and expectation, the glory of being an Englishman elating my soul, the happiness of my country gladdening my heart: but I had not travelled far before the day grew black with clouds, and storms and tempests gathered round about me. The howling winds made me their sport. Driven about by the jarring elements, I flee for my life from the violence of the storm.

I have long foreseen the consequence of the tempest that has been thus gathering round about us. Its savage force, spent upon the American coasts, has recoiled with ten-fold strength upon our own country, where it now rages with unbridled fury, and from whence it will drive the best and wisest of her people to seek refuge in the western world.

I shall

I shall receive the most sensible gratification, if, in the course of my remaining life, now dedicated to the service of a great and rising country, I can render assistance to my old and valued friends in England. The most salutary advice in my power to give them is, to prepare early for the event by some similar association to that which I have recommended. Their principles will be safe — their future lives will be peaceful and happy.

The name of Englishman shall not die! It shall live in the manners, the customs, the forests of America. It shall receive the awful remains of English Whigs, "*ultima Romanorum*," whose principles were coeval with the first inhabitants of the American States. These shall again mix with their descendants, who, equally jealous of their rights, have purchased their liberties at a high price — the price of blood.

*Si quando Tybrim vicinaque Tybridis arva
Intraro, gentique meæ data mœnia cernam,
Cognataſque urbes olim, populoſque propinquos
Epiro, Heſperia, quibus idem Dardanus auctor,
Atque idem caſus; unam faciemus utramque
Trojam animis; maneat noſtros ea cura nepotes* **.

If, as the illuſtrious Wanderer tells us, I enter America, and cultivate her fertile fields — if I behold her numerous and buſy towns filled with the Engliſh name, the common origin which gave us birth, and the misfortunes which ſeparated us, and which have driven me from my native

---

* If e'er the gods, whom I, with vows, adore,
Conduct my ſteps to Tiber's happy ſhore;
If ever I aſcend the Latian throne,
And build a city I can call my own.
As both of us our birth from Troy derive,
So let our kindred lines in concord live,
And both in acts of equal friendſhip ſtrive.
Our fortunes, good or bad, ſhall be the ſame;
The double Troy ſhall differ but in name:
That what we now begin may never end,
But long to late poſterity deſcend.
     Dryden's Virgil.

home,

home, will never be erased from my remembrance. The same religious attention shall descend to my posterity. Even the name itself, planted in a new land, shall render it equivocal to future ages.

Certus enim promisit Apollo
Ambiguam tellure nova Salamina futuram *.

But I am now saluted with the cry of land — the low shores of the country present themselves to our view.

——— humilemque videmus
Italiam, Italiam primus conclamat Achates.
Italiam læto socio clamore salutant †.

* Another Salamis, in foreign clime,
  With rival pride, shall raise her head sublime.
        Francis's Horace.

† ——— from far, like bluish mists, descry
  The hills, and then the plains of Italy;
  Achates first pronounc'd the joyful sound,
  Then Italy the chearful crew rebound.
        Dryden's Virgil.

I must,

I muſt, therefore, take my leave of you. I do it by committing you to the providence of GOD, who, in the midſt of the raging of the tempeſt, ſaith unto the ſtormy waves, " Be ſtill."— Farewel.

From on board the Britannia, in
  ſight of the coaſt of South
  Carolina, Dec. 2, 1784.

THE END.

www.ingramcontent.com/pod-product-compliance
Lightning Source LLC
Chambersburg PA
CBHW030257240426
43673CB00040B/988